I WAS A SUCCESSFUL
SINGLE PARENT

YOU CAN BE ONE TOO

I WAS A SUCCESSFUL SINGLE PARENT

YOU CAN BE ONE TOO

by

Ginger Lum

ISBN: 0-7596-0285-9

This book is printed on acid free paper.

1stBooks - rev. 06/06/02

DEDICATED TO MY GIRLS

This book is dedicated to my three girls, Terri, Traci and Tamalani. They have given me constant joy and a purpose in life. So many times when I worried about having enough money for us to eat, they made me forget my worries and laugh. When I thought I needed a man to love me, they would do something to make me boast about them, so I would forget my desire for a man. Primarily, I want to thank the girls for making life worth living and now giving me something positive to write about with the hopes of helping others.

Terri is now 35 years old. She skipped two grades when she was in elementary school. She graduated from high school at 16, and pharmacy school at 22 years of age. In high school, she played volleyball and basketball. She was a cheerleader, and she was an Honor Roll student. All the girls liked her very much and I had to chase the boys away. She attended Baylor University and later graduated from the University of Kansas as a Pharmacist. Terri is pretty with her brown hair and petite figure. She dated a fine young man, named Guill, for eight years and they have been married for twelve years. Guill is in International Business and Terri works one day a week as a Pharmacist at a San Diego hospital. Terri spends the rest of her time raising their two children, home schooling and helping her husband in his business. Terri and Guill are a Christian couple who sincerely care about others.

Traci is 31 years old and graduated from Pepperdine University. In high school, she played volleyball and basketball. Traci was a cheerleader and still managed to remain an Honor Roll student, graduating eighth in her class. Traci is always smiling, which shows not only an outward beauty, but an inward beauty. She won the highest honor for any student her senior year, the award best representing the ideals of the school. It was an honor voted on by students and faculty. Later, she went on to Pepperdine, where she was a cheerleader there, too. Traci married a nice, intelligent man, Jeff who also graduated from Pepperdine. They both worked at excellent jobs in Germany and Amsterdam for five years. They now live in San Jose with their two children where Jeff works in the computer business in the Silicon Valley. They, too, are a Christian couple who want to live the right life and show love to other people.

Tamalani (also called Tami) is my youngest daughter. She is 23 years old and in her second year at Pepperdine Law School. Tami took all Honors classes and somehow continued to play three sports all four years of high school: volleyball, basketball and softball. Her favorite activity was ice skating. Tamalani was always very active and a leader in her church youth activities. In high school she was a Peer Counselor and she was always reaching out to help other teens. She even taught a class to middle school children, on how to handle peer pressure -- she discussed drugs, sex, grades and reputation. All her classmates seemed to love her. Tamalani was Senior Class President and sang for her Baccalaureate. She is always singing and her beauty shines like a light to others. Since she was six years old she has said she is going to be the Chief Justice of the Supreme Court.

To you, my girls, I say thanks so much for making me the proudest mother in the world. You have done so well; I wish and pray for your continued success and happiness. I will always be here when you need me. I promised to never interfere where it is none of my business. I love you. Let's always stay close friends with one another.

I WAS A SUCCESSFUL SINGLE PARENT

You Can Be One Too

This is a book of encouragement to the parents of the 53% of children in the United States who are growing up in Single Parent homes.

Table of Contents

FOREWORD

I am writing on behalf of Ginger and her book on single parenting. As a professional who deals with these issues regularly, I know there has been a need for a book like Ginger's that speaks directly to the experience of the single parent without the usual jargon of the professional language.

In short, I believe that her book fits a needed gap in the literature - namely, what do you do with the particular circumstances of parenting. Ginger addresses them directly and sensibly. But best of all, she has lived them.

Sincerely,

David C. Bock, Ph.D. (PSY 4163)
Pasadena, California

INTRODUCTION

Perhaps you've picked up this book because you're scared. Possibly you have recently become a single parent. You just don't know how you will ever accomplish it all alone. On the other hand, maybe you have made the choice to have or adopt and raise the child by yourself. You are excited and still apprehensive. Conceivably, you could be a grandparent or a relative who has just been given the custody and responsibility of raising a child by yourself. You want so much to do it right. It's a scary world out there and you wonder what you will do to make your child different from all the others about whom we read and hear so much negative.

All these feelings and thoughts are normal. Even if the circumstances appear to be ideal, every new parent has these same concerns. I have never talked to a parent who didn't want to do the best for his or her child. We all start out with the best of intentions. Nevertheless, sometimes events appear in our lives that get us off the main track.

The intention of sharing my personal experiences with you is to encourage you. For the majority of my child-raising years, I have been a single parent. I have had very little trouble with my children. I have enjoyed the girls -- particularly those teenage years. We have all had fun. My girls love and respect me.

There is no doubt in my mind that it is easy to be a single parent. If your child is a baby, you might not notice this right away. However, when your child becomes about six or eight years old, you'll see the freedom you have in being a single parent. **Now before I go any further, I want to tell you that I don't think it was intended for any child to have to grow up in a single parent home. It would be a perfect situation if a child had both parents living in the same house and everyone**

got along without dissention. I wish I'd had this type of family for my girls, but I wasn't that fortunate. Apparently you aren't either and you and I are going to have to do it on our own. Therefore, I want to tell you in this book how you can take the, not so perfect situation, and turn in around to be very positive. You need to think of the positive points in being a single parent. You will be able to find more of these points in the single parent home than in the double parent home. You must change your thinking for the sake of your child. You can't sit around and think you can't do anything because you don't have a spouse. You can be a great single parent and if you will really make the effort you will no doubt be better at being a parent as a single person than if you had a spouse. Just think about it: If you had a spouse, you would probably leave many of the decisions to him or her and much of the time the child would be spent with the other parent. What if they don't do things the way you think are the best for your child?

Do you remember how it was when you were growing up? Do you recall the times your parents would disagree and even argue about a rule for you? Haven't you heard many a parent say, "Well, his father says he can't do such and such. I don't really see what harm it would cause." Or you have heard the father say, "His mother is so over-protective. She's going to make a sissy out of him." Except for finances and in-laws, children are the next major cause for disagreement between married people. A mother thinks she should give in and allow the father to make the final decision. After all, dads and husbands are supposed to be right; they are the stronger -- the smartest. We have been taught that. Besides, if one parent doesn't want to have an argument they often won't even give their opinion as it would be in disagreement with the other parent. A wife might think 'if I let my husband do it the way he wants and if the kid turns out bad, I won't be to blame.' Or often the husband is so busy trying to keep the family out of debt that he doesn't spend any time thinking about what is best for the child and he leaves it to the wife. He thinks 'Well, I'm so tired from all the decisions at work. I don't want to fight with the wife. She is around the kids more than me. I'll just let her make the decisions. Then, if the kid turns out bad, she can't blame me. I'll tell her, 'It's your fault. I wouldn't have let him do such and such. You were just too lenient. (Or, you were just too strict.) Doesn't this sound familiar?

The purpose of this book is to tell you how you can raise your children alone by taking the disadvantaged situation and turning it around to be positive. I will show you how raising teenagers can be fun. I will give you examples of the decisions I made with my girls, but the intent of this book is not that you have to do just what I did. The intention is to let you see how you can make your own decisions and be at peace about your child.

With my children, I made all the decisions. Yes, I knew I'd be responsible for how they would turn out when they were grown. Therefore, I had to think things out carefully before I made a rule. I couldn't blame anyone for a wrong decision, so I had to plan carefully. I didn't have to argue with a spouse. If I made a mistake, hopefully, I could catch it soon enough to correct it. There wasn't anyone pointing to me, accusing me of making the mistake. I didn't have to compromise on my beliefs, morals or values.

Allow me to just briefly tell you how I became a single parent. I was married at almost 21 years of age. I didn't attend college. All I ever wanted to be was a "good wife and mother." My father was a preacher, and being the good wife and mother is what he encouraged me to be. After my marriage, I soon had a precious baby and I was so happy. I gave it serious thought as to how I would teach her and love her. After four years, I had a second child. My husband was a flight instructor. To everyone who knew us, we seemed like the ideal couple. We found out our oldest daughter, Terri, was "gifted," and she skipped two grades. The second one, Traci, won the Healthy Baby Contest for all of Hawaii when she was two years old. We were happy. However, at the age of 28, my husband deserted us. I took him to work one day and when I went to pick him up, he had disappeared. He took nothing with him, no clothes, no trophies, nothing. I was in shock. However, I immediately thought of Terri and Traci. I didn't know what happened to my marriage. Maybe that had failed, but I wasn't going to let the raising of my children fail too.

As a new, young, single parent, I made some definite decisions. I will share these with you in each chapter. You don't have to make the same choices with your children that I made. Hopefully though, you will recognize how you, too, can raise your children to be happy, obedient, loved, secure and educated.

Just for the record, I did have another short marriage, five years later. As I tell people, 'I don't do too well with husbands, but I am fortunate that I do well with children'. You notice I am not writing a book on having a successful marriage. I'll leave that one to you.

Please read this book with an optimistic attitude. You CAN enjoy your children and be a Successful Single Parent.

YOUR CHILD FOLLOWS YOUR PATTERN

All children are going to pattern their lives after someone. Usually, it will be the parents, or with whomever they spend the most time.

When Terri was born, I was thrilled. During my pregnancy I hadn't thought much about child rearing. I was too nauseous to think very seriously and my only concern was to get that baby born. I spent those nine months trying to stay well enough to be a good wife. However, to this day, I can remember the actual moment I held Terri for the first time and I remember thinking 'What do I do to raise this little baby to grow up feeling secure, loved, smart and as pretty as she can be?' I wanted to do everything to make her the most well rounded person possible.

Even to this day, there is much discussion as to what is most important in creating one's character -- is it our heredity, or environment? First, I began to think of my hereditary traits. My childhood had been a very good one. I felt loved and I was happy. My mother says I was almost always a good child. Never had I really disobeyed or caused my parents heartache. I wondered why. Why hadn't I rebelled like other kids? What gave me that need to obey my parents? Why did I want to make my parents proud?

The first thing I did as I held my new little baby was to call my mother. I asked, "Mother what did you do to raise me so I turned out like I did?" She kind of stammered around. It was obvious she hadn't given any real thought to it. She had just done what she thought was right. I had hoped she'd give me a pattern to follow. I wanted an outline. However, she was unable to be specific with any help. I sat there, cuddling my baby continuing to think.

1

My parents had been very strict, but we, also, had many good, hard laughs. They would always listen to me when I had anything to say. My dad would take me with my friends anywhere we wanted to go. I always knew they loved me and they constantly let me know how proud they were of me. My parents loved each other and they showed it. Oh, they argued, but I never once doubted that they loved and adored each other. Mother and Daddy were a handsome couple. I could be proud to introduce them to my friends or to bring friends to my house. There were many positive things that I put in my memory, and knew I wanted to do this with my child.

It was then necessary that I think about the things I didn't like about what my parents had done. I was determined to learn from what my parents had done that I didn't like. I would not do the same things. One saying that I would bet you heard from your parents was, "When I was your age. . ." As a child I dreaded hearing that and I promised myself I would never use that phrase. I would never say, "When I was your age, I walked three miles. . ." Or I wouldn't say, "When I was your age, I worked. . .". The very moment I thought to myself; 'I will never say that,' I was reminded of parents whom I had heard say, "Yeah, my parents used to do such and such. I told myself I'd never do it -- but, I have. I'm just like my dad or my mom. Probably all parents say those things." Why do all parents have to say those things? I believe it's because they don't try to be conscious enough or don't make the effort to not say the same thing over and over, generation to generation. I wanted to try to break this pattern. In my mind, I vowed, I would think about what I said before I said it. This was an area in which I succeeded. Never have I thrown that saying in the girls' faces. I didn't have to tell them how things were when I was a kid. They are smart and remembered their history studies. My daughters know they have more modern conveniences than I had when I was their age. When we sit around and talk, I share stories of the past and we all laugh. I didn't find it necessary to put a guilt path

2

on them trying to convince them that their lives were easier than mine. Maybe because I was almost astute enough to know that while some things might make life easier for my girls, there are probably just as many things that make life more difficult.

A habit that my sweet mother had that I HATED was one I swore I would never copy. If I would ask my mother, "Can I go here?" She would react immediately and say, "No, you can't!" I would think every time that if she only listened to the details, she might let me go. It's true. Every time, without exception, I would continue and say, "But, Mother, please listen to the details. So and so will be there. We're only going to do this and that. I'll be right back." And Mother would always say, "Oh, O.K., you can go." Why didn't she listen before she reacted? I told myself never to react without hearing all the details. I have succeeded in this area, too. Many times the girls will ask, "Can I go here tonight?" In my mind, I wanted to jump in and say, "No, you certainly can't. You have homework; You were out last night; I don't like those people; It's a school night;" but, instead of saying those things, I kept calm and would say, "Tell me the details. Why do you want to go? What kind of homework do you have? Who will be there? How are you getting there? I thought you didn't like that person." I listened to the answers. I kept an open mind. Maybe it was for a special project, and they needed lots of help. Perhaps it would only be for a few minutes. I listened carefully. I would think quietly to myself, would this hurt my child? Could she get behind in any of her responsibilities? Perhaps it would make her feel good to be involved or help out? Would they be good people for her to become better acquainted with for future relationships'? If I felt comfortable with her answers, I would give my permission. If I didn't feel it was necessary, I would object. However, I wouldn't yell and make the child feel foolish for asking. I always knew I wanted to keep that communication between us. If I would yell, talk down to her or embarrass her, then I was certain she would quit talking to me. I thought about myself. Even now, if my

3

parents or friends make me feel stupid or embarrassed for mentioning something, I clam up and don't want to talk to them again. I consciously thought, this is just a little child. She doesn't know what is right to ask or do, like I, as an adult, am supposed to know. Asking questions and communicating is what makes people smarter. Therefore, I want to instill a confident pattern in her life that she can ask any question. I will always listen to the whole story. Never will I make her feel stupid. She will always know it's all right to ask me anything she wants without fear of being scolded. Perhaps she won't get the answer she wants, but she should ask. I want to keep the communications open. My child will always know I am fair.

Now, let's look at this situation if you were married and if you were still raising your child with your spouse you couldn't control your spouse's reactions. What if your spouse answered the child's question with a statement like, 'no, absolutely not!' Perhaps they would say to the child, 'that is a stupid thing to say.' Very possibly he or she wouldn't be as concerned and think as much as you about the future of your child. You won't have to be upset because your partner hurt the child's feelings. How many times I have heard one parent say to another, "Honey, why did you say that? That only hurt their self-esteem. That embarrassed them." Then the married couple ends up fighting, as the spouse gets defensive. Now, as the single parent, you know that only what you say and how you react is going to be seen and heard by your child, so you can do it in a positive way. So many people think there isn't much a parent can do to plan for the future of the children. They think all kids are going to go through various stages. Even good parents have bad kids. It's just a lot of luck, what friends they choose or what life deals to them. This type of thinking is what keeps parents from making any special efforts in child rearing. Don't think like that! Instead, be aware of what you say and how you act with your child. You want your children to grow up happy, secure, loved, well adjusted and educated. How will that happen? Anybody can, more or less, make plans for the child's education or finances. A bank, a financial counselor or a school counselor can do that. But what about the emotional part? Only someone the child loves, respects and whose lifestyle they are able to see, can affect the emotional part. I know that while you are raising your children if you constantly think about how everything you say and do will influence them to be happy, secure, loved, educated and well-adjusted that when they are older, they will know on their own how to prepare themselves for their education and finances. Most parents don't even think about how the child will pick up on their patterns. No doubt, they think. 'Oh, nothing you can do will change them.' Or, 'they will outgrow it.' Now that you are a single parent, you can show your child the part of a pattern or personality that you think is the best for them. Can you see how it's easier to guide your child alone?

All my life, people who met me as a little girl would say, "You look just like your daddy." I loved him, so I was proud of that. He was a very handsome man. I wasn't too pleased with my big English nose, but I had to live with that feature. Then, as people got to know me, they would say, "Ginger, you have the Tyler personality. You got that attitude from your dad's side of the family." For the most part, I liked the Tyler personality. My daddy was a hard worker. He always followed through in doing things for people. Daddy would always write lots of complimentary notes, which encouraged people. He was a funny man. My dad liked to know what was going on in the world, and he had very high morals and values. However, there was one thing (besides the big nose) that I didn't really like about Daddy. I thought he had too quick of a temper. It's O.K. to get upset if someone has done something terribly wrong; however, I used to think Daddy got too upset with the little things. Why should he get so upset if there's a lot of traffic on the highways? Why did he get so upset if he took the wrong turn off the highway? Why did he get so upset with rude people such as waitresses and store clerks? I didn't want to let things upset me so much. I knew I

5

had the same tendencies. When I thought about this as I held that baby Terri, I thought I don't want to pass this pattern of frustration on to her. I consciously --to this day -- am aware of getting upset when it won't do any good. I remember thinking I don't want this Tyler characteristic to be passed on to my daughter. If I knew I had the tendency and I didn't want the girls to have the same, I better do something about it now. I knew I had to set a good pattern. I began to look at things differently. When I'd sit in traffic and I began to get upset, I'd stop myself. I said to the girls, "Well, I guess we're going to be late. I guess someone is trying to teach me to leave earlier. I hope no one is hurt in a traffic accident. Let's say a little prayer for them. Isn't this exciting to be sitting next to so many people? Let's sing a song or play a game." When I'd make a wrong turn I'd say, "Oh, look I took the wrong road. Oh, well, we've never been on this road before. This is exciting. We get to go on a new road. Let's look around. We're getting smarter by seeing something new." I tried to always make something positive out of what seemed like a bad situation. At these times, I really had to work at not letting my irritation show. It wasn't easy as my nature was like my dads, to get upset. But I'd remind myself, 'what do I want my child to remember about her mother'? Now, I have to admit to you that I still am not too good at keeping myself quiet when it comes to rude people. I have to tell you that in case you are ever with me. I really have a low tolerance for rudeness and lack of common sense. What I do try to do when I'm with the girls is to say, "Did you see what she did? I don't understand. Isn't it common sense that she would know?" In other words, I try to use this time as an example to teach my child something. I hope that I can use that example to my girls so they won't make the same rude mistakes. For example, I will often say, "If I were a waitress, I would smile and be friendlier as I'd think I'd get a bigger tip." By pointing out a trait that I don't want my girls to have, they've been able to see what's good and what isn't. There were many times when I wanted to give the person a piece of my mind or perhaps a little instruction, but then I would think if I did

6

this, my child would just see me as rude as the other person and what would they think of me. If I didn't lower myself to the other person's level, but used it as a teaching time instead, we all came away much more relaxed and less irritated in what could have been a very unhappy situation.

If you weren't single and you had a spouse who reacted differently than you, you would lose control of the pattern you're trying to instill in your child. If your spouse were your husband, and if he had a temper and got mad at the waitress, you couldn't do much about it. If you confronted your husband about losing his temper, he might get furious with you and you might have a big fight. What kind of example would this be for your child? Maybe your spouse could be jealous or insecure. Perhaps they would accuse you of something or make snide remarks. You couldn't defend yourself or say anything for fear of a scene. But your child would definitely be picking up those nasty patterns. Those could possibly be the last thought or example for the child for that particular event. But now as a single pattern, you can make the situation a learning time for your child.

If I could think about my environment and make some changes, you can too. You have to want your children to be better than you are. When I slip up, I tell them, "Please don't get upset like mother did; it doesn't do any good. Why do I think I can change someone? Please learn from me, and be different." I know I've succeeded, because none of my three girls have tempers. Oh, they're not little weaklings, but they seem to have good judgment about what to say and when. They are definitely better at controlling their emotions than me!

While I continued to nestle my baby, Terri, and after I was through thinking about the hereditary part, I then began to think about the environment I wanted as an influence on my daughter. I knew I wanted her to have a good education. I didn't go to college; I was just told to "be a good wife and mother". That is wonderful; however, it was obvious that, by the time the girls were grown, they would need to have a college education in order to get a job. As important as getting the degree and book knowledge in college, I thought that there was a whole world of learning by living away from home and making decisions on your own. As I had not attended college, I really knew nothing about the preparations. It seemed obvious that in order for the child to get into a good college he or she would have to be smart. How would I make her that way? How would I instill the desire in her heart to go to college? My teaching would begin now. First, I could teach simple things. She would know that learning could be fun and positive. I read a book titled, "How to Give Your Child a Superior Mind," and found it simple and possible for me to do. I wasn't a big reader, but this book was particularly fascinating; it gave me guidelines on what to teach Terri. When she began school, each day I'd take time to ask to see the homework and I'd praise her. When I was a kid and when Terri started school everyone always thought girls couldn't do as well in math as boys. I wondered why and thought perhaps it's because we keep telling them we don't expect them to be as smart in math as boys. I decided to change that pattern. I made a special effort to ask about her math and I would always be positive and say, 'isn't math kind of like a puzzle?' and 'you are so good at math'. Even if she only got an average grade in a subject, I would remind her how smart she was and how proud I was of her work. She didn't have to get straight A's to be smart. And I thought that if I kept praising her she would feel better about herself and want to do even better. I always went to the PTA meetings and other school functions. I would look at the schoolwork she did in her classroom and I'd come home and tell her how proud I was of her work. They weren't always A papers or even B's, but my thinking was that there isn't anything she can do about "that" paper or assignment, as it's already been done, but if I let her know I'm proud of her, maybe next time she'll do even better. Isn't that true of you? When your friend or boss praise you and tell you that you are doing great work, don't

8

you want to try harder to please him or her? Don't you enjoy working better for them when you know they like your work? Also, my children always knew I would attend their school Open House or any school event. I wanted them to know I cared enough about what they were doing at school that I'd be there and see their work and always visit with their teacher.

I knew I wanted to be an example of happiness to my children. If my children were happy, not only would they feel better about themselves, but also more people would want to be around them. When I'm around people who are happy, I become happy. I decided to try to always be happy, no matter what had happened at the office that day or no matter what bills I feared I wouldn't be able to pay. Hopefully, my children would pick up on this characteristic. Once I had heard a friend of mine say she always remembered, when her mother would say good-by as she left for work or left her for school, that she would always smile. I thought, 'what a nice memory of a mother.' Wouldn't it be nice if my girls had that memory of me? I would try to have a smile for my children when their heads turned my way. I would do my best to always be a happy.

My thoughts then began to think about the dangers for youth and the temptations to do wrong, particularly when they would become teenagers. I began to think of all the dangers involved with alcohol. There were stories of people hurt and killed as a result of alcohol. I didn't want my children to be in a car wreck and get killed. I had seen people, who drank to excess, and it had ruined relationships -- it had wasted money. I began to think how difficult it is to grow up in this world, even if you try to everything right. I didn't want little Terri to do things that it seemed obvious wouldn't have a positive purpose. I thought, 'I don't want Terri to drink or to smoke.' I asked myself how would I do this. And I thought that if I didn't want her to do drink or smoke, then I better not do it myself. After all, she's going to follow someone's patterns and it probably would be

9

mine. How could I say one thing and do another? If it's not a good habit for Terri, how could it be good for me? I wouldn't need to do it either. I wanted to be the best example I could be. You can do this as a single parent. You can make the decision to not do anything you consider a bad habit. Conceivably, if I had been married, I would have had a spouse who would have thought drinking was O.K. - - perhaps only a casual drink. I thought about that. A casual drink might not hurt me. But how could a young girl know how to set guidelines? We adults don't learn a lot of guidelines until we're quite old. Certainly a teenager couldn't know how to stop and handle a casual drink. So I thought I better not start drinking myself. I better not have alcohol in the house to make it a temptation for Terri. I was afraid if she ever started with a casual drink she might like it and not be able to stop. That casual drink could perhaps get her killed or allow her to kill someone else, or just ruin her future plans. I would set the example. Should I want to have that casual drink, I could certainly wait until my child was grown and out of the house. That seems like a small sacrifice if I want to raise a happy safe child. I did ask people why they drank and would most often be told that it was because they had more fun or felt more relaxed as a result of drinking. I therefore, decided that if that was the case, I would instill in my children how to have fun and be relaxed without alcohol. I didn't want them to think they should have that drink to give them more courage or fun. Because of this attitude I took on myself, I have been told by many, that I didn't need alcohol to have fun. They thought I was crazy and courageous enough without it. Now there aren't many people who share my thinking about not having alcohol in the house and the chances of two spouses thinking the same way would be slim. If you were married, your partner might want to have those drinks and then you'd always be worrying what pattern your child will develop. However, if one of your decisions is to not have or wait to have alcohol, then you can do just that. You don't have to have it in the house as a temptation for your children. You can make this choice as a single parent. It worked for me and later for the girls.

Another pattern that has been invaluable to me has been the practice of believing in God. It has been important for me to believe there was a God who loves and cares about me. When I made mistakes, I believed God still loved and forgave me. When I didn't get what I wanted, it was necessary for me to believe that God loved me and would allow me to have something good or better later on in my life. When death or disaster happened, I believed God knew all and would give me the strength to get through it. When I had temptations, I had no doubt that God could give me the courage to pass them up. Therefore, I knew immediately that I wanted to give my child the belief in God. I felt I had to live it as an example. I wouldn't just send her to church; I would go with her. It gave us another common ground of things and people to talk about and events to attend. This is one of the secrets of being a successful parent; having more things to talk about with them.

I could give this Christian belief to my children because I made the choice as a single parent. If your spouse didn't believe in God, you might not be free to even mention God without hearing a snicker. As a single parent, you can make the decision. The obvious fact is that, without a spouse, you can make the decision you want without having any dissention from a spouse. There will be no controversy.

Can you see how it will be easier as a single parent to set a good pattern for your children? What a relief to know you only have to worry about the example you lead. You don't have to worry about the example of a spouse. You probably don't think his or her example was too good in the first place, or you would still be married. Ever thought about that?

THE SECRET OF SUCCESS IN DISCIPLINING

It's quite amusing to me that some parents think I was too strict with my children while others think I spoiled them. How can this be? What causes the difference of opinion?

When Terri was just a few days old, I vividly remember thinking about how I would discipline her. I asked myself how I could do it so she would obey and not hate me. It would kill me if she grew up to be rebellious. More than anything, I wanted her to grow up loving me. I wanted to enjoy her and relish every moment. Even as a young mother of 21 years, I could remember always hearing adults complain about their child and especially their teenager; I didn't want to be that kind of parent. I wanted to enjoy my children. Like many other parents, I read some books on disciplining. To be honest, I'm certain that during this last generation parents have been so concerned about discipline that they've read too much Dr. Spock and Freud. Parents have spent too much time with a therapist and being psychoanalyzed. It's strange, but so often the so-called experts don't have children who have proven their method as being the correct way. I didn't want to read what some PhD or minister wrote -- I wanted to know what really worked.

I noticed how many times other parents would threaten to discipline and then never follow through on correction. I would watch their sons or daughters reactions. A parent would yell, "Stop that, Johnnie." Then the parent would continue with his or her conversation with the neighbor. After a few minutes, the parent would glance at the child and notice he was still doing what he was told to stop doing. "They would yell again, "Johnnie, I told you to stop doing that." Then they would go back to the laughter and newsy bits with the neighbor. This process would continue throughout the parent's and neighbor's conversation. The threats and yelling didn't stop until the parent was ready to go, and she'd get Johnnie by the hand and say, "We've got to go now." That's it! The child never obeyed. The mother or father never followed through. The child never really knew he did anything wrong. I would often sit and observe the child while the parent was having their conversation with the neighbor and calling out threats to the child. The child wouldn't even look up and acknowledge the demands. The child seemed to be letting the threats just fly over his head. It appeared that the child didn't even really think the parent was talking to him. He just ignored them. Well, why shouldn't he ignore the parent? There didn't seem to be reason to stop. I decided that I would be different from those parents. It just seemed to me that being interested in talking to adults and my desire to hear that juicy story or watching a television program couldn't be more valuable that taking the time to correct, advice or instruct my child. I would never have that very moment again and I was smart enough to know that after 18 years basically I wouldn't have more chances to plant those seeds. I realized there would be plenty of time after my child was on their own that I could just visit all I want with my friends. I could watch T.V. all day with no interruptions if I wanted or I could stay in bed one morning and read the best book ever published until I got to the end. Now though, I would take these next 18 years to try to not miss an opportunity to guide my child. Therefore I made the decision that when it was necessary to discipline my child I would seize the opportunity and just politely ask that neighbor or friend if I could get back to them to listen to that situation or story; perhaps I could call them when my child was taking her afternoon nap.

The other practice many parents have is the "counting" method. I can hear you snickering now. Every one hears these threats to kids. "Johnnie, if you don't stop doing that, I'm going to count to three." Time goes by. Dad now yells "I'm going to start counting. Oonneee!----Ttttwwwwooo!!----I'm going to say three. You better stop. Ttthhrree! O.K., boy are you going to get it when you get home." That's not discipline! That's making a

14

fool of yourself. It's embarrassing enough to make a fool of yourself in front of an adult; however, you can't be too bright if you don't mind making a fool of yourself in front of a six-year-old. If you make these threats in front of me or any other adult, you're also making us roar with laughter inside. Do you like that?

At the age of 21, and holding a baby, which was just a few weeks old, I decided that no child was going to make a fool of me. I already knew the secret of success in disciplining. The secret is consistency. This took common sense. I didn't have to read Freud or Dr. Spock to determine the secret of disciple. I could just look around at teens and see what made the difference from one to another. Another even better thing to keep in mind, is the knowledge that if you remain consistent in discipline through those first six years, you will hardly have any problems of discipline with your teenager. You will enjoy that teen -- I promise you! It worked for me with three teenagers. Consistency doesn't cost anything, but it takes time and a lot of thought. You must be conscious of every threat of discipline you give. You must be able to follow through on what you say. Whatever you do, don't threaten a punishment if you can't follow through on it immediately.

The system of consistency I used was simple and I used it every time. The first decision I made was to not show anger or a temper when I punished. It seemed common sense to me that a little baby or child doesn't know what's right or wrong. Sometimes, it took me, as an adult, two or three times to learn something. I would be patient with my little ones. Even if they disobeyed for a second time, I would not get angry. Definitely, I would punish them, but I would not get angry. I don't like it when people get angry with me. I don't mind if they tell me I'm doing something wrong, but please don't tell me in a nasty way. The way I would discipline my girls was that I would first tell the young one, "Traci, you can't do that. You must stop." If she

15

continued, I would say calmly, "Traci, mother told you to stop doing that. If you do it one more time I will have to spank you." (I'll tell you how I did the spanking later.) Thereafter, if Traci continued to disobey, I wouldn't say one more word. I would stop whatever I was doing. I would take Traci by the hand and lead her to the bathroom or a room of privacy and spank her. She couldn't beg or cry and get me to change my mind. I made this decision on how to discipline when the first baby was born. I wasn't going to let a child make a fool of me. Oh, sure, every time they did something wrong, I wouldn't want to punish them. They were so cute. They were basically good girls. They were my only happiness, since I didn't have a husband. I didn't want to make them cry or feel bad. Still, I always thought of the commitment I made to consistency. I had seen so many teenagers who grew up to be very disobedient. They rebelled. I believed it was because of a lack of consistent discipline. They had no respect for their parents because they had seen the parents never be consistent when raising them. These same parents usually just reacted without listening to circumstances and then the child could ignore and talk them into changing their mind. I didn't want this to be the way my children grew up. Therefore, when I started to get weak and not want to punish my child, I would tell myself, 'If you stop now, Traci will never believe you in anything. She very possibly would grow up to be disobedient and rebellious as a teenager like all the others I'd seen. Don't let your child make a fool of you like many of the other parents you know'.

It has become very evident to me that the reason parents don't discipline their children is because they are afraid their children won't like them. Parents seem to think if they tell their child 'no' their child will hate them. I can tell you that if you know all the circumstances and still think the answer should be 'no' - your child will not grow up hating you. Kids often wish their parents would say no and help them out of a difficult situation. They can't admit it to you but so many times they

16

don't want to really go out with their friends because they know they have that project to do; or maybe they don't like all the kids that are going. However, their peers have begged and begged them to go, so they have promised to ask their parents. Of course, if you tell them 'no' they are going to immediately react because no one likes to be told 'no' to anything. It's human nature; face it - you don't like to be told 'no' either. Think about when you present an idea to someone and you are so enthused. When the other person doesn't agree, you and I immediately react and our feathers get ruffled. However, if we just will let ourselves settle down and think or listen to the other side of the story we will many times agree that our idea wasn't the best or the only one possible. Your child will be the same. Besides a child can never admit to even himself that he'd rather do something practical or even be alone than to go with their friends. But I can assure you that your child will appreciate you not always giving them their way. They will respect you so much more. Don't you look at your adult acquaintance and often think 'gee, that person has no guts; he or she is such a wimp; they let everyone push them around'. Well, what makes you think your child doesn't think the same of you? Now, of course you have to know all the circumstances and think things out clearly and be very open minded and should you have to tell them 'no' tell them calmly and briefly explain why. Don't go into a full detailed explanation and irritate them with all your talk. Just say "no" and mean it.

In these days whether to spank or not is a real big issue in the world. I know from what Tami has told me in her Peer Counseling instruction that a teen can easily turn their parents into the authorities for spanking. But I believe if you spank in the correct way and that you show more love and time then just being mean and hitting with anger, you won't have any problems. If all manner of discipline you do is done through love and patience your child will grow up loving and respecting you. Think about how you feel about an adult who is in leadership

17

and has rules. Haven't you always really respected the teacher, coach or whomever, who you would say was strict, but they were fair and treated everyone the same and with respect. Well, isn't this the way you would like your child to feel about you?

When I spanked, I used a little hibiscus switch on the little girl's legs. I never hit on the face or arms. I never did it in anger. I made the decision to do this, and I could because I was a single parent. I didn't have to consult with a spouse. I read in the Bible where God says to "not spare the rod and spoil the child." I interpreted that to mean that we are to spank our children. I knew I had been given a lot of spankings, as had my brother, when we were children. I seriously thought about the effect if had on me. I asked myself if I hated my daddy. No way! I always loved him dearly. I always knew I deserved the spanking and that daddy only did it when he had to make his point because I hadn't obeyed. Daddy never did it in anger. He just took me to the basement, had me bend over, and used that belt, but only on my bottom. He never just hauled off and hit me. He never hit me across the face – no where but the bottom and always in privacy. Before he spanked me he would ask me if I knew what I had done wrong. He made sure I recognized my disobedience. After he spanked me he would leave me alone and tell me to come out when I was ready to apologize. Well, it seemed to work on me as well as for my brother. We love our parents dearly. We are well adjusted with no bitterness. I was always a good girl. I never really did bad things and I believe that is because I learned at an early age to understand that rules were meant to keep and to have respect for authority. It was evident to me that my daddy followed the Bible's instructions and it worked; I would make the same decision with discipling my children. I knew I would be responsible for what I did. I had to make sure I had thought this out thoroughly. If the system didn't work, I couldn't blame anyone but myself. You, as a single parent can make these decisions for yourself. Perhaps you, too, think that you would like to use the switch from the bush outside. Maybe your husband would have refused to spank. As a single parent, you are at liberty to do as you want. Many hours are spent by husbands and wives arguing about how to discipline, but you won't have anyone to argue with you. Trust me -- it's a wonderful feeling. You must be willing to think it out and take all the time that's needed to make it work. You get to do what you want. Just make absolutely certain that you're consistent.

My aunt and uncle always talk about a time when I had to discipline Traci while they were visiting us in Hawaii. We were driving around, seeing the Islands. Traci was about five years old, always my little one full of tricks and entertainment. She was being silly and acting up in the back seat of the car while I was driving. I was trying to visit with my relatives. I said, "Traci, please stop acting up. I can't talk." She kept it up. In about 30 seconds I said, "Traci, mother told you to be quiet so I can visit. If you don't stop, I'll have to pull the car over beside the road and spank you." I didn't yell. I was calm. But I meant it. Well, she couldn't wind down. I waited about 30 seconds and I just pulled the car over to the side. I had a little switch in the trunk. I just calmly asked her to get out of the car. She knew she couldn't scream -- my girls knew from the beginning of their lives that wouldn't work with me; it would probably mean they'd get more switches. Because of the way I disciplined the girls, they always knew they were wrong. They couldn't help but think I was fair. I didn't yell. I gave them ample warning and didn't just lose control and hit them. They always knew I loved them. The times I wasn't having to discipline, the girls knew I would go out of my way to show my love and give them my time. So, this time, I spanked Traci beside the car. Then I knelt down beside her and reminded her of what she had done wrong. I told her I loved her. I then told her that she had embarrassed me in front of our relatives by not obeying me. As we walked around to get in the car, I told her she needed to say she was sorry to our aunt and uncle for disrupting. She did! I forgot it immediately! We had a great rest of the day!

You must be confident that if you tell your children you're going to punish them and if they don't stop doing whatever they're doing, that you have the time and space to punish. For example, if I was at a wedding or a funeral, it would be very difficult to stop immediately and punish the child. In this example, I wouldn't threaten. I might whisper that when we got home I would punish her. On the other hand, there was one time I remember that I had to take Traci out of church and go to the bathroom and spank her. She wouldn't be quiet. I threatened her. I just whispered, "Mother warned you. Now, come with me, we're going outside. If you cry or make any noise, you'll have a harder spanking." She knew I kept my word. I was consistent. She knew she better be as good as she could be. I did spank her. I explained things to her. I told her I loved her and I took her back into the service. Common sense told me that if I didn't take her back into church she might think, the next time she got bored, 'Hey, if I act up, mother will take me out and I can play in the yard.' I wasn't going to let any five-year- old be the boss of my family.

Sure enough, just when you are having the best visit with your friend, your children will act up right when you're in the middle of the most exciting conversation. You really want to keep talking and just ignore the child - just for 10 minutes. These are the times when it will be difficult to be consistent. Regardless, just remember, I'm promising you that if you'll be consistent on every occasion, you'll have wonderful teenagers. When your child is good, you must always praise him or her. Many times, I would say to one of my girls, "You were good in church this morning. I was proud of you." or "You were so good to let Mother just talk and talk with her friend. I don't get to talk to her too often. I was proud of you." Then I would add, "When we get home, I'm going to read you a story as a reward." Always let your children know you saw the good and appreciated what they had done. If you do this consistently from when they are

20

little, they'll grow up loving to make you proud and happy. When someone tells me, "I saw your daughter today; she is such a nice girl," I say, "Thank you. But more important, I go home and tell my daughter, "I saw Mr. so and so, and he said you're such a nice girl. That makes me proud." I often add, "I feel sorry for other parents, who can't be proud of their children. I'm so fortunate." Can't you just imagine how good my child feels? Think of your child as you think of yourself. You love it when someone compliments you; you want to do whatever brought on the praise again and be even better. But if you don't start the discipline and praise early, you won't have anything to praise those children for when they get to be teenagers.

When Terri was a little baby in her walker, she would love to walk her little self over to the television and try to touch the characters. I was married then and her daddy would holler, "Don't touch that!" I would think about each 'don't' or 'stop' I'd hear. I'd ask myself if they were really necessary. It seemed like there were so many forbidden things. I thought: If it doesn't hurt my child or the item, why would I have to say "No"? I wanted to save my "No's" until I really meant it. If I said "No" too much, I was afraid that they'd just stop listening. Accordingly, I asked my husband, "If it doesn't hurt Terri if she touches the T.V.,-- and it's very large and heavy, so she can't knock it over -- is it really harmful? She can't hurt the television. Do we have to stop her from trying to touch the screen"? All it did was dirty the screen with fingerprints. I cleaned the screen. I was willing to continue cleaning. I could see why Terri liked to touch the screen, it almost looked like it was a learning experience as she was trying to touch and follow the characters. That would have been an easier decision to make if I had been single parent. I wouldn't have had to be concerned about a conflict with my husband.

The secret with a toddler is to say "No" once, then promise to punish, and then to be sure to punish. Don't ever forget to be consistent! A time that you will get lots of practice with this training is when that toddler wants to touch something he or she shouldn't. Tell him or her 'No,' then caution and then punish. If you do anything three times you'll never have to do it again. Remember, it might be difficult to stop sewing or working on that car, but if you do it now you won't have to do it when he or she is a teenager.

As the girls got older I could continue to make my own decisions about discipline. It was easy. I treated them how I would like to be treated, but they always knew I was the boss. No matter how much respect I had for them, things weren't equal -- I was the boss, the head of the house. As the girls became teenagers and they asked me if they could go somewhere, I would listen to all the details. If I said, "Yes" they always said, "Thanks, Mom." If I said, "No", they'd say, "O.K." They knew to never beg. They never got mad. They never were allowed to sass back. I wouldn't even let them give a huff or a dirty look. If they did, I would punish them. I would just calmly add another punishment. I have often said, "O.K. I heard that. Because of that, you can't watch T.V. tonight." That's it! As I had always been consistent, from the time they were toddlers, and never backed down on my word, they knew they better not try to talk me out of it or make excuses. When I gave a punishment, I had thought it out and I kept to it. There were times it hurt me to say they couldn't watch T.V., because maybe there was something special coming on that they or we had planned to watch. Still, when I thought of backing down, I was reminded that if I did, I showed my child I was weak. They weren't dumb. They would know they could talk me out of anything. I had to be strong. I kept my eye on the future.

From the beginning of that child's little life and all through the teenager years, you must have control. Why shouldn't you? You're the older one. You're the parent. You should know more. You pay the bills. If all this is true, then please tell me why so

22

many parents give the control over to the kids? Kids need to know that the parent is the expert and speaks with confidence. When we have to go to the doctor with a bleeding cut, we don't want a doctor who faints or gets sick. We feel comfortable and are satisfied if we know he is confident. We don't want the doctor to be afraid to sew up the cut just because it will hurt for the moment. We must discipline while knowing that it might hurt our precious child for a moment, but he or she will grow up being a healed, whole person. We must act with confidence. That is why you have to really think and make sure of the decision you make. Once you make it, don't change your mind.

You must never let your children make you feel guilty. Don't let them tell you that such and such happens because they don't have a mommy or daddy. Don't let them make you feel guilty because your house isn't as nice as others or your job isn't as impressive. If they should say such a thing, just tell them you're sorry you can't give them that particular thing, but remind your children of what they can feel good about. Don't handle the problem with emotions. If you become hysterical and raise your voice you lose all control -- serious problems can arise that could affect you and the child for years to come.

Do you realize that I never had a curfew for my teenage girls? Oh, yes, I was very strict. They thought I was lenient because I didn't tell them when to come home. But I had my ulterior motives and instead of giving them a time, I had them call me after the dinner or after the movie and at that time I would listen to what they were planning to do next and then I'd set the time for them to be home. I told them sweetly, "Just call me after the movie or dance and tell me what you plans are for the rest of the evening." This way I knew exactly where they were and I had a chance to make a decision. Now, of course, I had to be home when they called, but this is just another decision I made in order to raise them in the best way I thought possible. I wanted to know what they were doing, without them thinking I was checking up on them. If my daughter called at about 10:00 P.M. and said the movie is just over and they're going to eat, I'd ask "Did you like the movie? Thanks for calling. Well, let's see. If you're going "there" to eat, the eating will take about an hour. It will take you about 15 minutes to get there from the movie theater, and another 30 minutes to come home; so, why don't we say you should be home about 11:45 P.M."? They're always very cheerful and say "O.K., Mom." I think they were actually excited to call me and tell me about the fun they were having. Almost invariable her date would holler into the phone in the background and say "Hi mom". Their friends never minded the fact that they had to call. Maybe it's because I knew their friends and was always friendly and kind to them so they seemed to like me. By doing this, I knew where the kids were all evening. If a parent just says, "Be home at midnight," he or she has no idea where the teenagers are going and what they're doing. I know these kids. Many times the kids get through seeing the movie and eating at an earlier time, but the boy knows the girl doesn't have to be home until midnight, so he will keep the girl out and they don't know what to do so they end up parking and you know the rest of the story. There is another excellent reason why we parents of girls need to ask them to call home. We need to give them a chance to get out of a tight situation. There were several times when Traci would call me after a date and when I answered, she seemed pretty quiet. I would say, "Traci, are you having fun"? If she answered enthusiastically, that was fine, but there were times when she would answer with "It's O.K." I would get the hint as I could sense she wasn't enthralled with her date. This reaction from her, no doubt, meant that she wasn't having a very good time and wanted an excuse to get out of the rest of the date. I would very quickly say, "You know, Traci, you've been very tired and I'd like you to come home right away." She would be relieved and say, "O.K. Mom." I was her alibi. She had been looking for an excuse to get away from this guy or group of friends. You know how difficult it is when we adults are with friends and we are bored or irritated with some

24

rude people, but we can't quite find the excuse to leave. Well, teenagers have the same desires and difficulties. They are younger and have had less experience than we have in making excuses to leave. Therefore, it's good that we can help them out. After all we have used our kids as excuses to leave a party many times, right? Didn't we all often say, "I've get to get home to the kids or the babysitter".

These are examples of the way I was able to handle situations because I was a single parent. I got to make my decisions, and I never argued with anyone. I could think with a clear head when my child called. I wasn't distracted with a spouse in the house and I could pay attention and listen to my daughter. It was a wonderful feeling. It's an advantage I had because I was a single parent. It's even a better feeling to know that my way worked, because I never had any trouble with my teenagers. The teenage years were my favorite.

One more thing I've noticed. All my girls turned out basically the same. I hear most people say that all their children aren't alike. Practically all parents say they have one child who is more difficult than the others. Well, I don't think that has to happen. I think it's because we, as parents, don't realize it, but we've handled one child differently from the other. Parents will always say 'I raised them exactly the same way". However, I don't believe that has really happened. It's hard to spend as much time or be as consistent or praise a second or third child as much as when you only had one child. I have no doubt that you think you did, but it's only reasonable to say you probably just couldn't. The only reason I know I did was because I was aware of this experiment with my girls. I was conscious of doing the exact same thing. My oldest daughter, Terri, is more serious. Traci, my second, was full of personality and loved to tease and be ornery. Tamalani's personality is somewhat of a mixture. Nevertheless, because I praised, punished, and tried to give them all the same amount of time, they've all turned out the same.

When I say they are the same, I mean they all are brilliant with excellent college education, they are all athletic, they are all Christian girls, they all care about others, they all love each other and aren't jealous or envious of each other. It would be very difficult to do this if you have several children, especially close in years -- that is just something you have to recognize. Wonders will happen, though, if you're just conscious of everything you do.

Granted, as a single parent, you'll often stand alone with your punishment decisions; however, the relief of not arguing and the rewards of thinking things out and having the time to be consistent will be far greater.

CHORES -- RESPONSIBILITIES

The area of chores and responsibilities was one that caused many disagreements between my husband and myself when we were married. All of a sudden, when I became a single parent, I felt a relief as I could now handle the chores for the children as I wanted. There wouldn't be anyone to fight with me. No one would criticize me.

Chores happened to be an area where I wasn't really certain which direction to take -- I was confused. I had always seen kids have certain jobs, such as taking out the garbage or doing dishes; those kids seemed quite well disciplined. I thought about my own childhood years, pertaining to chores. I had never had any real specific, regular tasks. I do remember daddy yelling to mother from the living room, "Let Ginger do it. She's going to grow up lazy." Mother would give me something little to keep me busy and be respectful of daddy, but I never had any REAL, regular duties; that was one of the things my dad got most upset about while I was growing up. However, when Saturday came around and mother cleaned house, I was usually around and I helped dust or whatever she wanted me to do. As it became close to dinnertime, I would find myself wandering into the kitchen to ask mother what is for dinner. I'd end up talking to mother, setting the table and chopping lettuce or something for that salad. It never seemed like work. I think I turned out all right. I now keep my house clean. I make sure everything gets done properly. I am by no means lazy. I wondered, could it be possible that daddy was wrong in this area and that a child could turn out good without the daily drudgery of chores? Could a child grow up without the daily stars on a chart routine and still not be a slob and irresponsible? It looks like it!

Then I thought of what I would like for my children. As a single parent, you can think about it and do what you think is best. You don't have to try to convince or argue with anyone. I knew I would be responsible for how I decided to handle this area of my children's lives. I wanted to do what would work the best in helping them to grow up to be the right kind of people. In everything I did or thought, it was my long range goal to ask 'what would be best for the children so they would turn out as the best individuals possible'. I knew I never liked it when I visited in someone's home and it was a complete mess. I definitely didn't like it when people were unorganized and irresponsible, so for sure, I didn't want my children to grow up like that.

I realized that I would like my child to help me when I needed it. I liked it when I offered to help my mother and she would tell me what she would like me to do. I would like my child to want to help me not because it's a MUST chore, but because she respects me and thinks she should be polite and offer to help. How could I get this to happen?

This is the choice I made: When the girls were barely able to walk, I would say "It's time for dinner. Would you help me set the table?" The child might only be about one and a half years old; I would say, "Here are four napkins. Please put them by a plate. One, Two, Three, Four". It isn't necessary for me to point out that the napkins weren't always on the left side of the plate, by the fork. I didn't want to discourage my helper. I wanted them to know how much I appreciated her help. I wanted her to think she was a good helper. I wanted her to think it was a fun feeling to help mother. I would thank her, praise her and tell everyone, "Look how nicely little Traci put the napkins on the table." I didn't make this an every night "have-to" routine. My feelings were if I made her do her chores every night, it wouldn't be a pleasure to help mom. It wouldn't be fun. And it would give children the idea at this very early age that helping and chores were miserable. So I would decide, if we were eating earlier and Traci was watching Sesame Street, counting, singing and learning, I wouldn't want to disturb her. There would be another opportunity for her to help and I didn't want to take her away from something that was fun and learning for her.

As the girls got older, I would ask them to do things like help me fold the clothes. If one day I got busy and was behind and I had to leave early for a P.T.A. meeting, I would say, "Terri, mother is running late. These clothes need to be folded. Is your homework all done? Would you please fold these for me?" And I can remember that often Tamalani would be on the phone, chatting away, and I'd just set the laundry basket in front of her and whisper, asking her to fold them while she talked. She never complained; she hardly knew she was working. In reverse, the next night, Terri might say to me "Mother, I have a lot of homework. I have a poster I have to make." I would tell her "Terri, you just do your homework and I'll do the dishes tonight." I treated my children as I would have liked to be treated. If we are working in an office, a boss will usually ask, "If you have the time, will you get this done for me?" Or the boss might say, "As soon as you are through with that project, please come see me as I have more things for you to do." That sounded like thoughtfulness, understanding and respect to me. I would like to have someone be considerate of me. I thought consideration would be the key in how I teach the responsibilities to my children.

As the single parent, in total control, I made the rule that I wouldn't have a regular time the garbage had to be taken out. If I wasn't too busy, I would do the chore. If I were busy, I would ask the girls to do it. They were NEVER allowed to sass me or give me a bad time if I asked for a chore to be done. On the other hand, I would be aware of their obligations. Many, many times, I would be rushing around, trying to get something done before I had to leave. The girls could obviously see my stress. I wouldn't want to leave them with all the work to do, so I would be trying to do as much as I could to get as much done as I could.

Nevertheless, the girls would say, "Mother, why don't you just leave the dishes? You'll be late. We'll do them for you." Do you see that even, as young girls, they were learning to be very considerate of me? They wanted to help. They didn't resent doing a chore. And, of course, I thanked them over and over when I got home or the next morning.

There never was a time I didn't thank and praise my children for helping me out. They knew I appreciated them. The rule was clear, though, that if they were late getting home from a sporting event and they had homework to do, that they were to work on their studies. I wasn't going to be nice and do all the work myself while they talked on the phone. Talking on the phone had to wait until their project was done; that seemed like common sense to me. They understood my thinking; I hardly ever had to remind them.

When I was married the second time, we were such a busy family. We wouldn't get home until about 8:30 P.M., after a volleyball game or meeting. My husband would argue that, "the girls have to do their chores, no matter how late it was or how much homework they had, or they won't turn out right." Well, they were in private schools, with a lot of homework and studies. They played two or three sports a year. They were involved in their church. I thought it would be considerate and best to let them study at night and get as much sleep as they could. The next night, when the evening might not be as hectic, they could help me in one way or another. My then husband didn't agree; the room would be filled with tension. It was so hard on me and made me very uncomfortable. I didn't want to disagree with my husband. I wanted things to be peaceful, but in instances like this, if I didn't speak up and have them do their homework, they wouldn't get started until real late, after the chores were done, and they'd be so tired they might not finish or get to bed at a decent time.

I feel I got the better deal out of handling the chores my way. Actually, I know I did! Because I was so considerate of the girls, they would go out of their way to help me when I needed it. So, many times, I got a lot of work out of them. More than my friends, who constantly seemed to be complaining about their thoughtless kids. Well, I think that even in chores, if you give respect, you'll get respect. I just didn't believe that responsibility could be imposed; I believed that it had to come from within their hearts -- it would come from the positive values that I would teach them. Observation had shown me that even gangsters and the Mafia carry out their responsibilities -- it all depends on where a persons values lie. I wanted my children's responsibilities to stem from respect for life and others. I couldn't just talk my children into values. They would have to watch and absorb my example. In order for that to happen, they would have to grow to love and respect me. I hoped they would notice that it is best to be considerate of one another.

If you are interested, all the girls, Terri, Traci and Tamalani are very neat and clean. They keep up their laundry. They cook (and I never got around to teaching them as, well, you know, it was busy and hectic being a single parent and some things just had to wait) and do an excellent job of it too. The house is always clean. My system worked fine.

Because I was a single parent, I did what I like. You, too, can make your own decisions. If you want your child to have regular chores, that is perfectly fine; they can still turn out to be very responsible. The main point I want to emphasize is that you, the single parent can make that decision; there will be no fighting in your home, no matter what you choose to do. Isn't that a great feeling?

YOUR CHILD NEEDS A PLAN -- A GOAL

At the time when I was a young mother, beginning at 21 years of age, I had no idea of what I was actually doing; however, I can see clearly now that one of the reasons my children have turned out so favorably is that they began having goals at a very young age.

No doubt, most little children are frequently asked, "What do you want to be when you grow up"? Most of the replies one will hear are "I want to be a policeman; I want to be a astronaut; I want to be a teacher; I want to be a doctor." If these comments are coming from your child, you need to follow through on these remarks. It's fun to listen to what that little person thinks would be a fun job. At this age, they're thinking of fun. This is O.K. More people should be working at jobs they enjoy. If they start to plan early, they could some day be working at the jobs they think are fun. Just because a job or career is going to take a lot of work or schooling doesn't mean it can't be enjoyable (that's the adult way of saying 'fun').

Talking to your child about his or her future can be a real pleasure, especially as a "Single Parent." You'll have lots of time to listen. When you're driving in a car and your child mentions a particular career that interests him or her you can take the time to discuss it openly. Remember when you were married and both your spouse and kids wanted to talk to you and you felt you had to talk with your spouse? There were so many times you wanted to discuss something with your child, but you had to give them a quick answer and tell yourself that you would talk about that subject with your son or daughter later. That "later" never came. When your child does bring up a subject, don't ever think 'Oh, I wish his or her other parent were here to help discuss this. I don't know the answer or what to say.' As I mentioned previously, I didn't attend college. I couldn't speak about careers or college like I had been there. However, my girls are proof that children only need to be listened to -- make them think and encourage them. You can even bring up the child's career dream when neither you nor the child realize it. As my daughters say, "mom is planting her seeds."

All little children (and older children) point to the Corvette, Jaguar or Porsche and say "That's the car I'm going to have when I grow up." Don't laugh at them and discourage them. Encourage them! Use that time to instill the dream and goal. Say, "Sure, you can. You're smart, and when you get through college and become a doctor you'll easily be able to have that Porsche." Then I would go on and plant a few more seeds by saying, "You just have to be patient and wait a few more years." As they became junior high age I would say something like, 'it's such a shame that some kids don't have the patience to wait for that *dream* car. Right out of high school they want a car so badly that they get a job, buy a car, start making payments and after paying for insurance, gas and maintenance, they hardly have any money left over to even go out. They like driving that little car and they don't even begin to go to college or they don't last past that first year. They have a job and they have a car. However, they end up buying just a 'regular' car. But, you, my child, be patient and get that college education and good job and you'll be able to afford that Porsche." Continue to make these reminder statements whenever the opportunity arises. By doing this, you're emphasizing your child's goals. Don't be negative when talking about a friend or classmate's new car. Just tell your child that if he or she remains patient and continues his or her high plans, he or she will soon have a car that's even better than the friends.

If you weren't a single parent, you very possibly would have a negative spouse who might think, 'This child of mine will never be able to afford that Porsche'. Your spouse might tell you not to encourage the child. They might tell you not to let them dream about something that is unattainable. I disagree. It's those

34

lofty goals that keep us working and going on. It worked for my Terri. I taught her that way. She went through six years of college on a moped. She graduated after six years, at the age of 22, and bought a beautiful, red Acura -- the first year they were sold. What did I tell her? I said, "See, Terri, you were smart. You were patient and got your college degree. Now you have an excellent job. You're only 22 years old and you can buy this beautiful, new car."

My youngest daughter, Tamalani, began talking to me about careers when she was only six years old. She said, "Mother, I don't want to be a pharmacist or doctor, because Terri is a pharmacist. I don't want to go into business, because Traci tells you she's going to be 'head of a corporation.' What other things can I do? I want to do something different." I thought about it. The first occupation that came to my mind was attorney. I said, "You could start with a lawyer's degree. Then you could go on from there. Many professions start with a law degree."

We discussed the law profession as much as we could. She asked about being a judge. I told her that first you have to be a lawyer. I told her there aren't very many women judges. Therefore, at the age of 6, she said, "I'm going to be the first woman judge on the Supreme Court." From then on, I began to point out women lawyers and judges to her from television programs and the news. I would say, "There's a woman judge." If a woman's picture should appear in a newspaper or magazine identifying her as an attorney or judge I would rip it out and show Tami. I didn't make her read the whole boring (to her) article. I didn't necessarily trim the article nicely. I just flashed it in her face to 'plant my seeds.' Within a few years, she realized she couldn't be the first woman judge on the Supreme Court. So she said she wanted to be the youngest woman judge. As she grew older, when asked, she'd say, "I plan to be the first woman Chief Justice of the Supreme Court." Whether she'd make it or not, I didn't know. But I believed that as long as she kept that goal in her mind she would have a very prominent position in some work field.

As a single parent, I can encourage Tami to be a judge whenever I want. I don't have to worry about a spouse being negative or trying to get her to do what he dreams for his child. When I was married, I often felt silly or too intimidated to suggest something to my daughter. Now, no spouse is listening to me. If I think it's important, I can say it. For example, when people would get nominated for a political position, they would be interrogated about whether they took drugs in high school. President Clinton was questioned. Potential judges were questioned. I would use this opportunity to "plant my seeds." I would remind Tami "Isn't it a shame that this person's whole career could go down the tube all because he thought it was the fun thing to smoke marijuana while in high school?" When Clarence Thomas became such a public figure because of Anita Hills' accusations I would discuss this with Tami. She knew that anything and everything she did might be brought up against her one day. I didn't have to tell her "Don't take drugs." She made that decision for herself because she had a goal. If she wanted to be a judge she had to watch what she did. She knew she was smart and could do anything. She didn't want to ruin it by a little peer pressure in middle school or high school. In fact, one day, I "planted more seeds." I told Tami, "Boy, if they ever begin to refuse lawyers a law degree because of taking drugs, there will be very few lawyers coming out of Carmel -- so many kids have tried drugs. Tami you'll be able to get that job because you've refused drugs." I feel free to give these examples as often as I want. No spouse is putting me down. No spouse is saying 'Oh, everyone is going to try it.' Don't you hear people tell you all the time that "All kids are going to experiment with drinking and drugs"? The kids overhear adults saying this. They think it's expected for them to try it. I dispute that saying. All kids don't try it! I didn't try drugs and Terri, Traci and Tami didn't try drugs. They knew I didn't expect them to try it.

36

Having these conversations with your child doesn't have to be a major discussion. You shouldn't sit the child down to talk and get too serious -- just seize the opportunity when it arises; news in the neighborhood, on T.V. or from your friends are good occasions to "plant your seeds".

When the children were beginning to plan and dream of their career goals I would praise them for such high goals and then we would talk about colleges and have a goal to aim high. We'd meet college kids here and there and I would always try to take advantage to have the girls talk to them or at least meet them. I wanted them to know as many people that they could who were going to college so these people could have a positive input. Since I hadn't gone to college and was young when I had my first daughter, I didn't know exactly how to encourage the girls to attend college. However, in the '70's, even I could see that more and more students were graduating from college. It seemed obvious to me that employers would have to eliminate many of the applicants who didn't have college degrees. It also made sense that if employers had a choice of hiring employees who graduated from private colleges with the best reputations or graduating from an unknown or state school that was not highly rated, they would hire the graduate from the better universities and colleges. Therefore, I began to encourage my children to aim for a good private university. They would worry about how their mother could afford it. I told them not to worry; they should just apply. Things would work out. I was in sales and I would hope for the best. If I weren't successful in sales, then they could probably apply for financial aid. They would, without doubt, have to get student loans. I emphasized that it would be better to have student loans in order to graduate from a good school because then their chances would be better of getting that "good" job and with that good job it would be easier to pay back those loans. I said they might attend a school where tuition is almost minimal; but asked, "What good would it do to have a degree if

37

no one hires you?" I reminded them that it would take a few years to pay it off, but it would be worth it to have carved a better than average college education and degree.

Too often, a young person will attend a college near home to save money; and, almost as often, he or she will quit within a year or two. Part of the idea of going to college is to live away from home. Living alone -- being responsible for one's self -- is part of college education. Also, a young person will probably make his or her best friends in college. All of this should be discussed with your child as he or she grows. Living away from home to attend college should be part of a young person's goals. A goal doesn't just pertain to a job; it relates to the whole life cycle. Our complete circumstance is what gives the adult satisfaction. You can have a terrific job, but if you don't have good friends or if you don't know how to be out in the world, you won't be completely happy. Living at home and going to college is just like having a job. Getting that higher education should be as pleasurable as possible, or many will get discouraged and drop out. You can't forget the fact that after your children graduate from a good college the friends they make might very well be the ones who refer them to good jobs. Networking and contacts are the most important factor today. Each year this fact becomes more and more important because the economy is becoming tighter and tighter and many of our college graduates can't get jobs.

Contacts certainly helped a classmate of my daughter, Traci, and son-in-law, Jeff, after they graduated from college. Traci and Jeff were fortunate to receive excellent jobs in Germany upon graduation from Pepperdine University. One of their friends was having great difficulty getting work. Traci and Jeff were concerned for her and offered to help. They agreed to hire her and give her a job in Germany. We have to give our children examples like this and encourage them to aim for the best college possible. A few years later, networking helped Jeff.

When they were ready to move back to the United States, it was their college network of friends that got him that interview. We parents should try to influence our children to give 100% effort in applying for college. We need to inspire them to think about making future long lasting friends as well as that degree.

One's children should know it's important to have high goals in looking for a marriage partner as well. The children must have the highest self-esteem possible. If they truly feel good about themselves, they'll know they deserve the best person possible for a spouse. We need to gently remind our children of this. Marriage is one subject I felt inadequate to discuss with my girls -- I had failed with two. I really couldn't understand why my marriages had failed. There seemed to be no one who wanted to love a husband and children as much as I did. I had planned how to have the most successful marriage. I had thought it out. I definitely was sure I had done everything correctly, but neither marriage lasted. How could I give advice to the girls? Many times, I began to fear that the girls might even have some very negative feelings about marriage. Oh, I didn't hate men or talk bad about them. However, I worried that perhaps they wouldn't take marriage seriously. Maybe they might enter marriage thinking, 'If it doesn't last, I'll just get divorced.' I didn't want them to be flippant and casual. Marriage should be taken seriously -- it should last. What could I say to the girls?

At different times, I spoke to the older girls and told them they might date a young man who would be afraid to become involved in a serious relationship with them for fear they might think that divorce was an option. I apologized to the girls for the fact that they might have to defend themselves because of my divorces. I wanted them to understand that one often hears that if the parent doesn't take marriage vows seriously then the child might not either. I suggested that, should the girls get into this type of conversation with a young man, they could explain how mother hadn't believed in divorce. I had and still believe that

God intended for marriages to last. My only goal in life had been to be a good wife and mother. I had always believed that if I were a good wife then my marriage would last and be perfect. Well, it didn't happen that way. Therefore, I asked them to explain that their first dad almost had a nervous breakdown and deserted us. I wasn't able to control that divorce by desertion. I then asked them to explain that the second husband had beaten me up. I hadn't wanted divorce. I was just scared for my life. I believed that a marriage should last.

Over the years, I tried to point out why I thought my marriages hadn't lasted. I wanted to take responsibility for my mistakes and point out the errors to them. After all, my whole purpose in life was to raise these children to be happy, so I'd have to let them know where I thought I'd made a mistake. I decided that, no matter what had happened to my marriages, I wanted to try to help my girls make their marriages last. In order to do this, I felt it wouldn't be wise to always be blaming the husband. Maybe that husband didn't act in the right way for a specific reason. Perhaps I had not had enough self-esteem, or had married the wrong person. Instead of talking bad about their dad I would try to talk with them about how the marriage might have worked if I had done things another way. I wanted the girls to see what not to do. My first husband couldn't handle the financial stress. It really wasn't much, but he couldn't manage. I reminded the girls that I had become pregnant on my wedding night. I was very nauseous; and I couldn't work. My husband wanted to give me the best and perhaps he charged too much on credit. Neither one of us had a college degree. I explained to the girls that I honestly think if we both -- or at least their dad -- had a college degree, we would have probably had a better income and had more money. No matter what, it would have given him or both of us more self-esteem if he'd had a college degree. Their dad felt he had failed; as a provider because he couldn't give the family everything he wanted to give them and because he had to work seven days a week and wasn't able to spend

40

much time with the kids and me. If one has an education, it can't help but boost one's ego. In addition, I concluded that the girls should really try to prevent pregnancies for a while. The marriage needs to get on its feet financially. A new husband and wife need to adjust to marriage; then they should be able to save up money or buy the things they want, before they begin a family. I used birth control, but it didn't work. I hastened to tell the girls "Be careful of that foam stuff."

I was always willing to admit where I thought their dad and I had made mistakes. Perhaps the reasons for divorce are just because two people don't like each other. If that could be the situation, maybe, if they had waited until they were a little older, they would have realized they really didn't have much in common with the other person. Could it be that one or both doesn't have the self-esteem or confidence they need? Could it be they didn't plan and think things out too well? When I was young and thinking of the man I wanted to marry, I always thought I wanted to marry someone who had the same Christian faith as me so that we could attend church together. However, both men I married did go to church regularly with me and they were involved in the church, but I pointed out to the girls that just because we went to church together, it obviously didn't keep the marriage together. I told the girls that they must look for other things in a partner as my situation had proven that you must have many common interests and goals for your family.

Enjoy those precious times of "planting your seeds" for your child. As a single parent, you can plant all the positive seeds you want. No one will laugh or criticize you.

One lesson I learned in a very difficult way. Traci was such a darling girl; I was always finding good guys for her to date, but always in a joking way. As if she needed my help! She was always a good sport, though. However, my carefree, fun times led to disaster. Traci came home from Pepperdine her first

Christmas break. I met her at the airport with the information that "We have the cutest and nicest new youth worker at the church. He's the pastor's son. You'll love him. You'll meet him, as we're all going ice skating tomorrow night." As I said, Traci was always a good sport. She had plenty of guys. Well, she met Jim and agreed he was a nice guy. Jim told me within a few days that he had never liked anyone as much as Traci. I was elated. Jim was older -- out of college -- a secure, good guy. Traci knew I was thrilled. They dated and things moved extremely rapidly. Before Traci was to return to Pepperdine, Jim had asked her to marry him. He had given her a lovely ring. The three of us had dinner with Jim's parents and Traci decided to not return to Pepperdine and instead to attend a college in Hawaii so she and Jim could date. She flew to Pepperdine to get her belongings. Well, Traci hadn't even been back in Honolulu three days when she tearfully told me "Mother, it doesn't seem right. I don't love Jim." Fortunately, this time, I was smart enough to explain to her that it wasn't too late to back out of the engagement. Sadly, I realized that I'd been caught up in all the excitement of her finding a man who seemed to be the neatest guy, and I had probably pushed this potential marriage. After all, I loved his parents. By now I, too, had seen evidence that Jim wasn't right for Traci. She broke the engagement, and she certainly paid the penalty; she was so unhappy at the school in Honolulu that one semester. I felt terrible and I was so thankful that Traci pulled out before it led to an unhappy marriage. I learned a serious lesson and I would like to share it with you: Do not push any particular person on your children for a girlfriend or boyfriend or marriage partner! Wait until your children say they are in love and want to marry. Then you can be happy and encourage them. It just isn't wise to encourage someone for your child just because you like him or her. You are not marrying that person. Maybe you, like me, are divorced. If so, we need to recognize that we didn't choose spouses, for ourselves, too successfully -- so what makes us think we can choose our children's spouses?

We need to be positive with our kids in helping them plan their goals. We should tell them they can do whatever they want, as long as they're willing to work for it. They have to believe in themselves, have the right mental attitude, and have the right morals, so they won't make a stupid mistake and have their possibilities destroyed. As a single parent, we can "plant the seeds" and remind our children about these things daily. You can't wait until your children are 17 years old to sit them down to talk about their goals. You need to begin when they begin to talk. I always tell my child "Talk to your brain." If your mind starts to get worried or negative you need to "talk to your brain." Don't let the worries or negatives rule. It's the old water glass of half empty or half full theory. Sometimes my daughter would say "Mother, I know he was talking bad about me. He was looking at me and pointing." I would come back with the comment "He was probably saying 'look how nice her hair looks today'. Or maybe he was saying to his friend, 'She's the one who smiled at me today and was nice to me.' By making these comments throughout their lives, I was instilling a positive mental attitude. If my child was positive she knew she could achieve her high goals. If my girls would be worried about a test they had at school that day, I would remind them that they had spent many hours in preparation. I would tell them again how smart they were, and that I knew they would remember what they had studied. Then, when I dropped them off at school, I would tell them I would be praying for them at the very hour they were to have the test. This way, when she went into the classroom, the positive thoughts would enter her mind. She would think 'I studied. Mother thinks I'm smart. Mother is praying for me right now. I'll do it.' You can't wait until your child is a teenager to use these examples to be positive. You have to start when they are very young, so when they are older they'll believe you and know it works. It will be a way of life.

This positive way of teaching your child to reach his goals worked for my children. They didn't have two parents and they

43

didn't have a mother who went to college. Many years, we had very little money; however, I could talk, "plant my seeds" and be positive. I could tell them they could be whatever they wanted. But I also had to do what I could do to help. Just what could I, as a single parent, do? I couldn't get an education for them. I couldn't make them be positive, just because I told them. In my simple way, I decided I would teach them that they could be positive and do it for themselves. It takes time. I spent 18 years of daily taking the time to be positive and to "plant my seeds." You, too, can do the same for your child. You don't need a spouse to help raise your children to be positive and to teach them to know they can attain their goals. In fact, as a single parent, your children probably won't see any arguing with a spouse -- that in itself is positive. When something negative comes into your life, you can turn it around for your child and be positive. Be sure that when, whatever looked like a disaster, turns out O.K., you point out to your child and say, "See how things work out? Sometimes it looks like it's such a terrible situation, but look what took place because that happened." Traci even said to me, when she was 16 years old. "Mother, don't ever worry that you divorced dad, and I didn't have a dad. I know that because you were alone you were able to spend more time with me." She even noticed the positive at 16 years of age. She was able to turn around the negative situations of having no dad and my divorce to find a positive result. Bless her heart!

BOLSTERING YOUR CHILD'S EGO – SELF-ESTEEM

If you were asked what the number one problem with our youth is, you'd probably say it's the use of drugs. Perhaps you'd say its AIDS. Others might say the worst problem is drinking. And there would be some people who would say that violence is the largest and fastest growing problem. Others might say that the lack of education and motivation is America's biggest concern. These are all serious problems. They are all good answers. However, I guarantee that none of these are the worst problem your child faces.

A low self-esteem is the worst problem facing your child. It is the most tragic problem facing all children. I guarantee that if your child has a high self-esteem, you'll never have to worry about drugs, drinking, low grades or violence. I can't promise that on AIDS because, as I write this, there isn't enough evidence pertaining to that terrible disease. But a high self-esteem will help control the drive for sex outside of marriage also.

How can I make such a promise to you? Because I tried it out on my three children. My children never drank or took drugs. They got good grades. They weren't brains or nerds -- all three hung around with the "in" crowd who did these things. -- still, Terri, Traci and Tami didn't. Why? It's simple. I started when they were very small. I held that, one day old, baby and wondered what makes kids and adults grow up and have bad habits. What makes kids succumb to peer pressure? I thought it must be because they don't think enough of themselves to stand on their own two feet. The kids who succumb aren't leaders -- they follow friends. They're afraid of being laughed at by their peers. As I have mentioned, I wasn't highly educated and I hadn't read any special books about what to do. My thoughts turned to myself and what made me feel good about myself. There was no doubt that I thrived on compliments. They made me feel encouraged. If I felt confident about myself I could do anything. When I felt good, I could smile and be happy. At that moment, I made a commitment, when I held each of those babies for the first time, that I would give them the biggest egos I could. I would see if it worked. It did! Daily, when I was with the girls I thought of how I could compliment or praise them. I never once thought 'Oh dear, I've got to lecture and scare them to death about the results of drinking, sex, drugs and poor grades.' Because I made the girls feel so good about themselves, they made their own decisions about life. I beg you to try it with your child.

Bolstering your child's ego starts so simply; and it stays that way. You don't need a college education or a prestigious job to do it. You don't need money. You don't need a wife or husband to do it. It doesn't take a lot of time. It's fun to do. You can see the results immediately; and you'll see the long term results when your child goes on to college.

Just begin with praise. Praise that little baby every time you can. When he eats that icky liver, say, "What a good baby!" When he sits up, say, "You're so smart!" Tell your baby when you pick him up, "You're such a pretty baby." Those of you who are new parents are probably agreeing and saying, "I do that. This is easy." It is easy to do when your child is a baby. All babies are so cute and such a delight to have. We enjoy them so very much; and we continue to enjoy them when they begin to talk. We have so much fun teaching them to talk -- when they say those words and sentences we always beam with pride and praise them. The child sees that. They love to see us beam and they want to make us happy. But what is it that happens after that precious baby grows into a second grader and is in school? All of a sudden, they aren't quite so cute as they once were. We may think the teacher is teaching them so we don't have to do anything anymore. It's up to the teachers and school basically now. We know we've done a good job until now and now the school will take over. Also, we may begin to give the younger children our attention. We think what we do doesn't matter anymore. Subconsciously, we forget about much of child raising after the children get into school. Then, when that boy or girl gets into about 6th or 7th grade, we suddenly notice some changes we don't like: Their friends aren't the greatest. The school begins to send us warnings that children are now drinking, taking drugs and participating in sex. We panic! In fear, we try to talk to our child. We get involved in school- sponsored organizations to encourage kids not to take drugs. Our thoughts go back to our upbringing, and probably we think that maybe we should take the kids to church. Well, it's probably too late then! Once your children have picked up bad habits, they're most likely not going to stop until they fall on their faces, which might not be until they get into their 20's or even later. By the sixth grade, your child has basically learned his morals and values. He knows just where his self-esteem is. A parent doesn't have much influence on a child after the age of 12. I heard at a seminar once, that your child learns 80% of values, habits and morals by the age of 6. Then from the age of 6 to 12 a parent can teach them about another 10% and after the age of 13 you won't have a chance to influence them much more. If you're a new parent, please don't ever stop praising that child daily -- even through those awkward and not so cute years from seven to about twelve.

When your children begin school, and every day for the rest of their school years, always ask them how school was that day. If you ask, you must listen. When I picked up my girls after school, I knew that for about 20 minutes I had to just listen. Sure, it wasn't easy. I probably had things I wanted to tell them. Often, I'd even begin to talk and then I'd catch myself and say "Never mind. You finish talking. I'll tell you later." I mean, I'd hear all the 'rattling' on and on about the school day; but I paid attention. If one of my daughters said she got a good grade in math or

47

spelling, I would ask to see the paper. I'd ask to see the artwork. I would always tell her how proud I was, and how smart she was, even if she got a C or even lower grade. (After all, getting A's doesn't mean a child is smart and getting D's doesn't mean he's dumb. However, if the person feels good about themselves and that someone thinks they are smart, they are going to try harder and will do better.) Then my daughter would tell me instances that happened with teachers -- and then the kids. I paid attention, and tried hard to be interested. I often had to ask "Now which teacher or which kid was that? I forgot." Many times, I would have someone else in the car when I went to pick up a girl from school. I would politely warn my rider, "Now, when Tami gets in the car you'll have to excuse me because I will want to listen to all she has to tell me about school. She'll talk on and on, for about 20 minutes." My riders knew I couldn't talk to them until Tami was through. This too, boosted my child's ego. She knew I thought she was more important than my friends -- that I was interested in her. After I heard all the details, I would tell my daughter, in front of whoever was there, "You are so smart. That was a nice thing for you to do. Mom is so proud of you."

The crucial factor was that my girls knew I thought they were important people. If they felt I was proud of them, then they'd feel good about themselves. Whenever we would run into a business client or a casual acquaintance, I would always say, "Meet my daughter, Terri. She is so special to me." It seemed reasonable to me that if my girls knew I thought so much of them, they would realize how much of a disappointment it would be to me if they jeopardized my feelings.

It's necessary to never talk bad about your children behind their backs. Even if your children have hurt you or caused you disappointment, there's no need to talk to someone else about it on the bleachers at the next ball game. You wouldn't want your dirty laundry spread all over. That child of yours might be very embarrassed about a mistake he'd previously made and most importantly, you don't know when your children will overhear you, or if your comments might get back to them. I've had all three girls hear other mothers say, "Oh, my children give me so much trouble. I can't wait until they're out on their own. The teenage years are the worst. If I had known how difficult it was to have kids, I would have only had one." Each one of my girls, when they heard these remarks, have thought it was sad that a parent would talk like this. They asked me, "Mother, do you say those things about me behind my back?" Fortunately, I could look them in the eye and say, "Never." Whenever someone comes to me and says, "Oh, you have a teenager. What terrible years." I refute that person. I say, "Oh that's not true. I love the teenage years. The kids are so much fun." This is absolutely the honest-to-goodness truth; but you must raise them right in those first years if you want to enjoy the teenage years. By the time my girls were teenagers, they had high self-esteem. They knew I loved and was proud of them; and they could respect me because I treated them with respect.

As a single parent, it's so much easier to listen and praise your child -- this isn't even mentioning the fact that maybe your spouse isn't inclined to praise or be patient enough to listen. My second husband absolutely did not believe in giving compliments. His theory was, "You're my family -- you're expected to do what's right. You don't need praise for doing well. If you do wrong, then you need to be criticized." We never heard praise out of him; but we heard plenty of criticism. I'll never forget that at one dinner-time, when I was trying to keep the conversation going at the table, I said to Traci, "Traci, tell Dad what grade you got on your math." She said, "I got an A on my math final." Without raising his head, he replied, "Is that the best you can do?" I was surprised at his response and I said, "She got an A. She can't do much better than that." He replied, "She could have gotten an A+." Maybe you would battle the same types of comments if you weren't a single parent. Perhaps your spouse doesn't criticize, but maybe she is always talking to his or her friends, and doesn't take the time or care to listen to their child. These would all be negative signs that wear away at your child. You might think your child is too small and will never know the difference, but I am proof that this is the type of things that parents do and then they wonder why they are having trouble with their child, as they grow older. Now, because you're a single parent, it will be easy for you to instill only positive comments.

Your children can lose all of their self-esteem when they have disappointments in their lives. We parents need to spend more of our time building the children up when they get beat down -- we need to constantly be encouraging them. These little beings are our future. If they get their hearts broken and give up they will never succeed in life.

Probably one of the first disappointments your little child might have is when she doesn't get the friend she or he wants. Maybe the friend is mean to them. You need to encourage your child to make new friends. Perhaps you can help clear up a misunderstanding. Better yet, you can encourage your child to talk to that person and try to get things settled. You don't need to start blasting the friend because he or she doesn't like your "little Johnnie." Your child doesn't really want you to criticize that other child -- he or she will want you to help make it work. Listen to your child. Try to help him or her figure out an explanation. Teach your child to forgive. Remind them that Jesus says to forgive and if He can forgive us when we do wrong we certainly should forgive others. Teach your child not to be vengeful. As a single parent, you will have more time to help your child through this difficult time. You will have the time to listen. You don't have another personality in the household telling your child, "Leave that kid alone. He's a brat. You don't need him for a friend anyway." You know that isn't an attitude anyone should have. As a single parent, you want to begin at this early age to teach your child how to work out relationships.

Perhaps you can even invite the other child to go with your son or daughter for ice cream. You might not be able do this if you have to hurry home to a demanding spouse. However, because you are single, you can spend a few extra minutes with this young precious life you're molding.

Speaking from experience, a second disappointment that many children get is that of not making the sports team or not to be a "starter." Because you're single, you have the time to take children to the park where they can practice more to get ready for that sport. With Tami, I realized that as an eighth, ninth, and tenth grader, we had a serious problem -- she was determined to play basketball. She worked hard at practice. Not only was she short, but also she had not grown up practicing basketball. The other girls all had dads who practiced with them. Tami wasn't around any older man, and she was behind in basketball abilities. She knew how to ice skate competitively, but that's a very different activity. I couldn't ignore her determination to learn. I found out about basketball camps and I sent her. At one point, I didn't have the money. I asked if they had any fundraisers or financial help. The coaches told me they would give Tami a scholarship. We were thrilled! I reminded Tami that it was all the more reason she would have to work hard if they were willing to give her a scholarship.

Then there was the time at the end of her 10th grade year that she knew she would really have to work hard to be on the varsity team. I had even suggested that she not go out for basketball her junior year. I reminded her that she was short, and that there were many good players on the team. Why didn't she choose another sport? She's a fighter and adamantly refused to quit. Therefore, I knew that one of the boys' coaches opened up the gym for the boys after school. I spoke to him and asked, "Is there any chance Tami could come to the gym and practice too?" Woody was such a kind person; he responded, "Sure! I'll do what I can to help Tami. She's got strong legs and the potential to be very good. She just needs encouragement; and she's such a good girl." Tami was very excited. The coach spent a lot of time with her; and Tami improved considerably. He later told me "I can't wait to see the varsity coach's reaction when she sees how much Tami has improved." My child's self-esteem was bolstered; Woody's self-esteem was bolstered, because he got to help her; my self-esteem was bolstered, because I had done something to help my girl.

Traci had been a cheerleader when she was in her younger years. During her early high school years, we had moved to the mainland and she had not gone out for cheerleading; then we returned to Hawaii at the end of her junior year. She told me she would like to go out for cheerleading her senior year. However, she was sure the competition was so severe that she would not meet the judges' approval. I verbally encouraged her; told her to try, and not to be discouraged. But I knew I had to do more; she would need to make sure she had the confidence to compete -- I would try to get her private lessons in cheerleading. At that time, I had never heard of anyone tutoring anyone in cheerleading, but I thought, why can't I ask one of the University Of Hawaii cheerleaders to coach her? I would pay them. So, I did just that, and I called the university. They told me that no one had ever been asked to tutor cheerleading before, but they'd ask around The next day, a young man, who was one of the University of Hawaii cheerleaders, called me back and said he would be glad to teach Traci real quick. We went for a few lessons, and she got back in shape. He told her how great she was and definitely encouraged her. She went back to her high school and competed and she was one of the six girls chosen. She blossomed during that senior year. From then on, she knew she could do anything. I have no doubt that those few dollars and a little extra time built up her self-esteem so much that she began to glow and continues to glow until this day. She ended up graduating with the highest honor available that the school gives out, as she was voted by students and faculty as the one who best represented the high school.

There will be times when we have to depend on our words to build up our child's ego. I was very disappointed when Terri lost the title of "Homecoming Queen" by one vote. To make matters worse, she told me that a lot of kids didn't even vote because they thought she had it "in the bag." If I had been married, I'm sure my husband would have pooh-poohed this disappointment - - he wouldn't have thought it was important. I mean, Homecoming Queen is just a girlie thing - not important to most men. As a single parent, and one who really tries to understand and cares very much for her children, I could see how this loss could be devastating. I couldn't have repaired the damage if a spouse had not taken her disappointment seriously. Hopefully, I could use this setback to teach Terri a lesson. You can be certain she now knows how valuable it is to vote and to stand behind her friends. I had to keep reminding her that her day of winning would come eventually, and that she couldn't give up. We have to use these time of disappointments to keep planting those seeds to our children and reminding them that this is where our faith is necessary. I mean, who knows, Terri could have let the Homecoming Queen success go to her head and she might not have remained the sweet, humble girl she should be. We have to use these times to teach out children. Don't get mad at the world and at her friends. Encourage you child and let her know how serious her feelings are to you. Assure her or him that their "time will come to win" some day if they just don't give up.

Personal appearance is very important to your child's self-esteem. The girls and I have noticed this about other children over the years. The compliments about how attractive my girls were repeated regularly from outsiders. What made the difference? It couldn't be due to money as there often wasn't much available. I did always comb and curl their hair when they were little. They all had long hair. Every morning, before school,

I would put them in front of the television to watch cartoons, while I'd neatly comb their hair back, and pin it with pretty barrettes. Combing their hair before they left the house was a habit I was instilling, so, when they became teenagers, they would always want to fix their own hair to look nice. It has been proven that teachers give more attention to the cute and nicely dressed pupils. -- I had read that when I had my first baby. I decided to try it -- it's true. The girls liked the compliments they had received as little children about how nice they looked. If the style was for "permed" hair, I would make sure to find the money for them to get that permanent. I wanted them to be in style with the trend, and not to feel self-conscious. However, I had my limits. They never gave me any trouble. They knew I would find the money and do the best I could to keep them in style, but I wouldn't go to extremes. For example, I had my timing for the girls to get their ears pierced. Even all through high school I wouldn't let Tami have double-pierced ears. She never gave up on asking me and I'd sort of giggle about it and I'd continue to say, "no." After all, I kept thinking, we don't have enough money to buy earrings to fill all the holes and, also, I was afraid that if she had those ears double pierced, that all the rhinestone and glitter would draw attention away from her pretty face. The girls don't argue with me though, because they've grown to respect me over the years -- they know I want them to look their best. Because they have high self-esteem, they don't have to go along with an extreme fad; they know they're accepted as they are.

I do try to buy the girls good clothes. I might not be able to buy them lots of clothes, but I do try to buy them from the better stores. All this really depends on your situation, your neighborhood and school. If all the children at your child's school buy clothes from K-Mart then that is perfectly fine. If your child's classmates buy the brand name jeans then I think you should buy them brand name jeans. Sure, you can't afford five pairs; however, if you can buy the child one or two pair and wash them often, then these jeans will help your child feel better about himself or herself when he or she heads off for school. You need to listen to your child. Whatever it is that you think might be affecting your child, then listen to him or her. Make every effort you can to help him or her. My children would appreciate that I would buy them a couple pair of the more expensive jeans; then they would have cheaper skirts or shorts -- something that could do without brand name. You don't have to go overboard, but remember we're here to build up our children's self-esteem. If they appreciate our efforts and sacrifice, they won't ask for more. If they ask for more, then just simply remind your children that you're sorry, but you just can't afford more at this time.

I, also, set my own rules on certain new, faddish styles. I'll just give you a couple examples of decisions I made and hopefully it will encourage you and show you that as a single parent, you can make your own decisions and it isn't so bad after all. As I've said, in other places in this book though, if you do make a decision, you should have thought it out thoroughly and then you MUST stick to it. If you ever get wishy washy on any of your decision, your child will lose respect for you and your parenting will begin to "go down the tube." For a while it had become popular for little boys to have long hair with a little tail hanging down. As a single parent I would have chosen not to let my son wear hair like that. I could make that choice because in my mind having hair like that didn't prepare the child for growing up to look like a man and go out and get a job. It would be very unusual for a man with a tail down the back of his neck to get a job in the business world. I didn't feel that would be character building to let that son know he had to go along with every fad. The same is true for boys to have earrings. You are the single parent and you can make whichever decision you want, but you won't have to argue with anyone about it. On the other hand, if you take a stand about something you need to explain to your child why they don't need to go along with the others; then you must compensate in another direction so they do not begin to think they are weird and that, 'you just don't understand kids and you are so mean.' Perhaps you can buy them extra nice clothes. Maybe you can take them, more often, to the sports center or the video arcade. Maybe you would enjoy letting them bring the boys over and bake cookies and let them eat and watch T.V., without you hovering over. If you want to be a good parent you have to think! You have to think about the results of your decisions and how your child will feel. At first that son might be very upset that he can't have earrings or a ponytail, but if all the kids think his mom or dad is cool and they can go over there and lie around on the couch and eat chips and cookies and not be bothered, that child will be much more secure and soon will forget the disappointment. Think of this too; if you let them dress in the newest faddish style, that will soon be over and your son will have learned nothing. However, when you had to go to a little more work and take him and his friends places or let them eat in your clean living room and you had to clean it up, you were giving your son good feelings about himself and his home life. This is life lasting building up of self- esteem. It just takes a little more work, but it's worth it.

As a single parent it's much easier to help build up your children's self-esteem; you'll have more time. You won't have to divide your time with a spouse. You can listen. You can think about the advice you give -- it can be just your advice. You will make it positive. No spouse will be around to ignore the importance of the children's ego or to make fun or to even criticize. As you see your children grow with determination and confidence, you can be so proud and thankful that you made that special effort to give them the self-confidence they need. If you had to give much of your time to a spouse, who was perhaps a workaholic or maybe an alcoholic or one who just has a negative or careless attitude, you wouldn't be able to do so much for your precious children. Perhaps they would grow up not knowing they were loved and secure. Don't sit around feeling sorry for yourself that you don't have a spouse helping you raise your child. Very likely a spouse would not influence your child the way you think is best. Forget thinking about yourself. Help your child feel good. Spend your time bolstering your child's ego. Investing in bank accounts, real estate or bonds will never be worth as much as your child's future. If you don't invest in your child, you will, no doubt, eventually end up selling those investments of real estate and cashing in the bank accounts to help get your child out of trouble because you didn't take the time to build up his self-esteem.

DO YOU REALLY KNOW YOUR CHILD'S FRIENDS?

Don't we often hear the statement, "The parents tried to do their best, but their friends influenced the kids in the wrong direction"? Or have you heard it said, "They got in the wrong crowd"? Whenever I hear these statements, and others, I can't understand how that happens. Where were the parents all this time? You should know who your kid's friends are at all times!

It's easy to know a young person's friends. It's fun to get to know them. When you get to know your children's friends it gives you even more to talk about with them. Your children's friends give you examples of bad and good that you can use to "plant your seeds." This isn't even considering the fact that you could be of help to other kids who might be neglected and need a little attention, as they aren't getting enough in their own home.

Knowing your children's friends is one of the real advantages of parenting as a single parent. Seize this opportunity to know more about your children.

As a toddler, you let your child play with your friend's children in your yard and the park. Later, they go to preschool. You don't have to be too concerned about influence at the preschool. You take them and pick them up. They aren't quite old enough to get into heavy conversations. And then they're off to kindergarten, first and second grade. During these years, they're so excited about school. Practically all of their activities are happening at school. They don't get on the phone. Their birthday parties are in the classrooms, or maybe in your home. Mostly, the child is influenced by the family. However, there is a space in here where the child just sort of drifts away. Usually this happens sometime around the second grade, as they are growing into a little bit of an awkward stage. At this age the kids aren't quite as cute. Independence is beginning to show and they don't want to be hovered over by a parent. Schoolwork often becomes more difficult and maybe discouraging. They don't understand the importance of schoolwork over electronic games, cars, dolls or skateboarding. Being a parent can become a little frustrating with children at this age. But don't give up and definitely try to know their friends.

Begin to attend all your child's sports activities. If you see your child with a friend, ask him or her, "Is that your friend"? Tell him or her to, "Please introduce me." Be nice to the friend. Say something cute and silly so the friend won't feel awkward. Tell the friend "I saw you playing baseball. You are good." These kinds of statements make the friend feel good. They also make your child feel good; and it gives your child the feeling that he or she chooses nice friends, and that you are proud of him or her. As you continue to see this little eight,-- nine,-- or 10 -- year-old friend of your child's, always try to speak and give him a compliment. Invite him to the house or to go out for pizza with you. By being cordial, you are continuing to keep the communications open so that your child won't hesitate to have you meet his or her friends. Be careful! Don't be critical of these kids. They aren't going to be perfect. Hmmm! But if you're too picky or complaining about the little things of their friend, your child won't want to tell you anything about any friend any more.

If your ten-year-old should tell you his friend cheated on a test, you must not go off in a tizzy. Always think about how this situation can help your child. Use this example to "plant your seeds." Say to your child, "Oh, its too bad Johnnie didn't know the answer. I'm so proud of you for studying and knowing the answers. You are so smart." You see, if you go into a tangent and begin to lecture on how bad it is that this boy or girl cheated, your child will never tell you anything again -- you will definitely stop the communication. Remember, you're not responsible for raising that other child. You are responsible for your own children. Use all the negatives to point out the positive.

I definitely believe the crucial periods are the fifth, sixth, seven and eighth grade years. This is the time when parents lose control and communication. It is difficult, but you can remain in control. These are the years the children start smoking, drinking, taking drugs, having sex, losing interest in school and choosing friends who will be a greater influence on their behavior than possibly the parents. Personally, these are the years I enjoyed the least. My children weren't as cute as they were and they certainly didn't do all the cute little things little preschoolers did. I couldn't seem to talk to them about "girl things" as much as I could later, in their teen years. It also seemed that often, no matter how hard I tried, nothing seemed to make them happy. However, I stayed in there. It would have been much easier to just ignore them, complain with my friends, read, watch T.V, and just wait until they got past that stage. But I was concerned that I might not like the next stage if I didn't stay in touch with them during these years.

One big suggestion I'd like to give you is to try to always drive your car to pick up your children. Do everything you can to attend a game, ice skating lesson, piano lesson, P.T.A. -- just everything you can to be with them. It would be easier for you if they got a ride with a friend's parents or even if they took the bus, but you need this time with your child to know what is going on in his life. You have to be with them when it is not obvious. They will expect a parent to attend these activities. They'll think you're just picking them up in the car because it's the easiest thing to do. They won't realize you're really doing it because you want to stay in touch and see his friends. Offer to take your children and their friends to a game or movie. You don't have to sit with them when you get there. In fact, you should sit on the other side. However, you've still had the opportunity to meet and be with their friends while driving in the car. This is a real secret: Always drop anything you're doing to take your children someplace. Don't let them take the bus. Don't let them ride with an older brother or sister. DON'T do it begrudgingly. Be happy to help. So what if the lawn doesn't get mowed? So what if the laundry doesn't get folded? If you don't keep an interest in your children you'll have plenty of time to mow the law and fold clothes while they're in Juvenile Hall or out taking drugs because you lost control. I don't believe when you die anyone is going to judge you and say, "She really kept those clothes folded the minute they got out of the dryer." But I will bet you that they'll judge you by saying, "He sure did everything to show his children he loved them."

Because I stayed in touch and in open communication with Tami she has always known she could tell me anything and I wouldn't go hysterical. The perfect example of this was when she was in the eighth grade and I picked her up from Middle School when she said, "A boy asked me to 's _ _ k' him." Oh, boy, was I shocked! My hands on the steering wheel began to sweat. BUT - I didn't react. I told myself, 'Don't say anything until you think.' First, I thought of the positive, 'She told me, didn't she? I'll bet you that very few girls would even tell their mothers.' I was so proud of her for that. My second quick thought was, 'I don't want to react or I'll lose communication with her.' Thirdly, I thought, 'Gee, this is the same thing men say to me as a single person, only maybe they're a little more discreet.' Therefore, she's going to hear this type of thing for many years. For her to grow up to not hate men and to know how to handle herself, and be happy, I came up with the following answer: I replied to her, as we drove home, in a short and simple way. "Tami," I said, "You know you're going to hear things like this all your life. Men even say these types of things to Mom. You have to learn how to handle it without getting mad. You don't need to slap the guy. Boys and men just grow up thinking girls want to do this. It's up to we girls to control them. It's good if you can make yourself very clear with a little humor." Tami never likes me to dwell too long on any one issue. I had gotten just about this much out and she said, "O.K. Mom, you don't have to say any more. I'll handle it." I believed her (but, of course, I was nervous). I was just glad I picked her up every day and she didn't have idle time to be tempted to do these things. The next day, when I picked Tami up from school, I had more or less forgotten about the previous days conversation. Well, I hadn't really, but I didn't want to bring it up. Tami got in the car and I asked the usual "How's school?" She said, "Good! Jimmie asked me if I would f _ _ k him." Again, I began to sweat. The thought of going to the Principal's office came immediately to my head. But what good would that do? It would embarrass Tami. She would be known as a squealer. Kids would be afraid that, she'd report them to the school office. The Principal can't be around the kids every minute to protect them. I just need to use this opportunity to raise MY child. So I calmly said, "What did you say?" She said, "I told him I was going to wait for somebody who was experienced." I laughed and said, "That's a great remark. You put him in his place, with humor." This experience taught me a couple of lessons. First, I kept the communication open with my daughter. She isn't afraid to tell me things so I can continue to give my advice. Secondly, I was able to begin to teach her how to handle boys and men. Thirdly, we were able to discuss sex, and kids who have sex. As I said earlier, I could never talk too long at one time to my girls about something as uncomfortable as sex because before long they'd say, "O:K, mom, that's enough!" I always stopped immediately when they would say this and I'd just wait for another opportunity.

Very possibly you might not agree with how I handled this situation. That's perfectly fine with me. I only tell you to give you an example of how I've handled some of my parental predicaments. The main thing I want you to know is that, as a single parent, you can deal with all circumstances as you want. I just want to encourage you that if I could do these things as a single parent then you can do it too. You don't have to argue with a spouse who wants to do it differently. No doubt, if I had been married, Tami wouldn't have told me. She would have been afraid that I would tell her dad. I probably would have. Don't you just imagine that he would have stomped down to the school and ranted and raved? He would be sure to "take care of things." No one would talk to his little girl like that. (Well, dads and moms, let me tell you, kids are talking like that and you aren't going to be able to stop them. However, you can teach your child how to handle himself or herself). But, really, what good would that do? It would have embarrassed Tami, of that I'm sure.

Tami has continued to tell me everything that goes on at school. I'm always shocked, but I don't let it show. Instead, I make a sympathetic statement. I have often asked Tami, "Do the other girls tell their moms about this"? She raises her voice and says "No way, Mom. Their moms wouldn't know how to handle it." One day, Tami told me, "Mom, guess who I saw taking drugs the other day?" You could tell she was so hurt as she then told me it was a little 14 year old girl whom I really liked. She had been in our home a lot that past school year. She and Tami were good friends and played on the same sports team together. I had often mentioned to her that it was good Tami had a friend like her -- one who didn't drink or take drugs. I even "planted my seeds" with her. She seemed strong in her convictions. When Tami told me, I was so saddened. I said, "Oh, I'm so sorry, Tami. That breaks my heart." I didn't react with anger, but with sympathy. Tami relaxed with my response and said, "You know, I'm going to go call her." She did. She came back to me and said, "Mother, she said that was the only time she had done it. She feels so terrible. She says she's not going to do it again." Maybe Tami helped. If I had been emotional, Tami and I would have had a fight. She wouldn't have been in the mood to help this little girl.

When Tami was in high school she played three sports each year. She went to church and attended Young Life activities. She always needed a ride. I always took her. I would give up meeting with my friend, or watching a T.V. program, or doing housework, -- anything to help her. It's my investment. I never got frustrated for having to take her places. I practically always had a carload of other kids whose parents didn't seem to care where there kids were going. Many of the kids rode with their friends. It seemed like everyone in our area got a car as soon as they got a driver's license. I could easily have done what other parents did; and I could have asked Tami, "Can you get a ride with so and so? He goes right by our house"? I never said that. Instead, I'd just say, "Oh, Mom doesn't mind taking you." Many times I was exhausted, but I just told myself to take one day at a time and remember I am investing in this child's future. Somehow, I got through it all. This way, I kept control. I knew exactly where she was going. I often went to a little coffee shop and had coffee, wrote letters or read while she was attending her activity. I didn't go inside and watch and hover over her. I waited for her to come out. You see, Tami didn't realize what I was doing. She thought I just liked to be with her: and I did! But more importantly, I stayed in touch with her. I know what was going on and I got to see her friends all the time. I didn't give her the opportunity to get in a car and go someplace with the driver and hang around doing things that weren't right for a 15, 16 or 17-year-old. If you should choose to do this, as I chose to do, with your children, you have to make sure your children like being with you. Primarily, I mean you must not criticize or embarrass them. When Tami would get in the car, usually about five or six other kids would come running up, all excited from the events of the evening. They said "hi" to me. I always smiled and said something nice to the other friends. Then, when we left, I asked Tami if she'd had a good time. She'd tell me about the kids -- who did what and who said such and such. I knew Tami appreciated me being there. Kids love to talk if you'll just listen and not criticize or nag them. She never complained. I did this same thing with Terri and Traci too. Your children will appreciate having a parent who is interested in them. At least weekly, I had a child say to Tami, in front of me, "You're so lucky you have your mom." Kids want to be loved. They want attention. They want to know someone will go out of their way to do something for them. They are craving for these types of things. The rides to and from a place were often our most valuable time. We had lots of time to talk, with no interruptions - - no phone calls, no T.V. and no pressing homework or housework. Please, don't think and tell your child you love them, if you allow them to always get a ride with someone else so you can participate in your group or your personal activity. Show them you love them by being willing to put your personal desires aside.

When you're around your child's friends you must be sure that you look as good as you can. Kids get embarrassed very easily. This is called 'peer pressure.' As adults, we have peer pressure too. We should always try to be as attractive as we can for their friends. You don't want your child to bring his friend up to the car and you are dirty, sloppy or, worse yet, have been drinking. Many kids are afraid to take friends home because their parents will be drinking. If you have this tendency, you should really think about it. You must not think about what you want in life while you're raising children. You wanted those babies so badly. Throughout all their years at home you're suppose to be the best example. I don't care what kind of problems you have. We all have had, what seems like insurmountable problems. Still, you must think about having your children grow up loved and well adjusted. We don't want these kids to be emotionally disturbed, alcoholics, druggies or always coming back home to us, after they are once on their own, or to be always asking for money. They will have one type of problem or another, if you have been putting your interests first all those first eighteen years of that child's life. After the children are out of the house and are on their own, you can do what you want. Now is the time to put your child's interest before yours. You'll see the rewards; I guarantee it. Time goes by fast. There will be plenty of time for you to drink, work, go to the sports gym, read those books, and have sex, after your child has left the house, if that's what you want to do. But right now you must think of your sons or daughters first.

If you were not a single parent, you very likely couldn't spend as much time with your children, especially driving them all around or attending all of their activities. You'd have a spouse who wanted you to do something with him or her. You'd have to get the dishes done so your husband didn't think you were a slob. You'd have to fix the wife's car so she didn't think you were lazy. As a single parent, you have no one to worry about except those precious children. There is no pressure. Laughing kids can be so much more pleasure than other temporary things we once thought were so important. Knowing that you are giving your children a cheerful smile, a nice compliment and your time is a wonderful feeling. Those simple gestures and comments can do so much good for your child and his future.

HELPING YOUR CHILD OVERCOME PEER PRESSURE

Why are we parents so surprised that peer pressure has such a profound effect on our kids' lives? This is a serious question. We get so upset with our children when we realize they have succumbed to their peers – their friends. Why do we do that?

Think about your own life. Since you left your parents home and have been on your own, what has the most influence on you? Be honest with yourself. Could it be your friends; the people you work for or work with on a daily basis?

Why do you want to live in that particular neighborhood? Is it for health reasons? Or is it so you can keep up with your family and friends and be in as nice an area or better than theirs? Is it because you think you will have better friends or people with whom you would like to associate? Why do you want a newer, better or different car? Is it because the old one won't get you where you're going? Or is it because you want the newest trend in automobiles – one that is similar to the neighbor's or friend's car? Why do you want new clothes? Is it because you'll go naked if you don't buy that newest dress or suit that's in the window? Could it be because you want to be in style with your friends and the community? Why do you want to join a particular club or organization? Is it because you have nothing to do all day but sleep and you're trying to keep busy? Perhaps it's because your peers are members of that club. If you join, you will belong to the "in" crowd.

Do you see the peer pressure that kids are going through is nothing different than what we as adults experience? As adults, we have just learned how to disguise it or we don't recognize it. We make our reasoning sound intelligent. We say, "We need a new car for a tax shelter." Or "I want to join that organization to

69

be of help to the community." Ah, come on now! It's O.K. if you do all these things, just please don't be so critical with your children. Try to be more understanding with them. Your children just haven't lived as long as you have, so their decisions aren't always too good. They don't have money to do or buy certain things. Therefore, with their peers the pressures are of a different sort; they just hang around or, unfortunately, get bored and make some wrong choices. We, as their mothers and fathers are there, not to scold, but to help. Mostly, we should prepare them so they avoid trouble.

A lot of peer pressure problems can be solved by beginning when they are young, to guide them in choosing their friends. You have probably already read that chapter. The next step is to just be understanding; and, most important, we need to give those little children high self-esteem so they won't succumb and make the wrong choices.

We need to listen to our kids. At a very young age, if your child starts to ask you simple little questions about drugs or drinking, then that is the time to listen. Know they have more to say than what they are actually saying. Answer them simply and positively. If your child begins by arguing that drugs and drinking don't hurt, then you know they have been approached. They have begun to feel peer pressure and that can become very dangerous. Be encouraging and tell them that not everyone does take drugs or drive. Tell them the good that results if they don't participate. Begin to point out examples on the news and in the community of things that have happened because one didn't make wise choices – because one drank too much or took drugs. If you drink and they question you about your position, then you need to make a serious decision. Would it be better for you to stop so that you can be an example to your children? I think we need to stand with these kids. If all the world is against them, they should know that at least one parent supports and is behind them. I certainly would be willing to give up something, if only temporarily, to help my child keep away from harm.

Your child will probably want clothes that are of the newest fad 'because everyone wears them.' I think you should look at the style. It may seem different, but if it's not really too offbeat, perhaps you could buy them one or two outfits of the latest style. I mean, if you look back at what we wore as kids, aren't we rather embarrassed at those fashions? The main thing now is your child's self-esteem. We don't want our children to grow up as freaks, so they think no one wants to hang around them. I think that if I didn't want my daughters to smoke, drink or take drugs, then I couldn't refuse to let them do everything that all the kids are doing – as long as it wouldn't hurt them. I wanted my kids to be happy and strong, with lots of friends, so that perhaps they can be an influence to other kids by showing you can look "cool" and be fun, but don't have to take the drugs, smoke or drink.

When Tami was in high school she has always liked school. Each summer she could hardly wait until the summer was over and the next school year would begin. BUT -- no way were we suppose to tell any one that she liked school so much. Why? Because she didn't want to look like a nerd. "No one likes school, Mom." My natural reaction is to reprimand her. I wanted to scold her and say, "Don't be afraid to be honest. Stand up for what you think is right." But, hey, if this would embarrass her in front of her peers, I could keep this secret. It's not going to hurt her or me. She had a very busy schedule with all her sports, activities and schoolwork. She had a lot of books to read. We would run around a lot after school, and she would carry the book she had to read for that week in her English class -- she wanted to take advantage of every spare minute for reading. Nevertheless, when we would walk around, she would always sneak her book into my purse and ask me to carry it. She didn't want her friends, if she ran into them, to think that she was so

71

interested in studying that she carried her book around with her. She thought they'd think she was weird. She did like schoolwork and wanted to get good grades, but she was also a very social and athletic person. It always seemed a little silly to me, but I decided not to scold or lecture her on this little matter when I was concerned with bigger issues. It just seemed that if she didn't drink or take drugs, then I shouldn't worry about what I thought was so trivial. I wanted to use my time and energy for teaching her things or issues that we're larger and more serious.

I do think it is good to encourage our children to be different from the crowd. We do need to explain that they don't need to follow the group particularly when it comes to the major issues. In school Tami had so many kids who told her they couldn't believe she had never drank alcohol or taken drugs. She would repeat this to me and then she would tell me that someone had asked if she wanted to try it for the first time. Then, when she said, "No, thank you." They would answer with, "I can't believe you have never tried drugs or drinking. That is neat!" When she told me of these conversations, I would instill my encouragement by saying "Gee, doesn't it feel good to be different? Weren't you the center of attention? Wasn't that fun?" I asked her if it was hard then for her to say 'no' and she would say, "No; the kids actually thought it was neat." What I was doing was pointing out the fact that being different can really give you lots of good attention and it doesn't have to be difficult or embarrassing to say "No." Use these times, when your child makes a decision to stand alone and not to follow the crowd, to praise them and tell them how proud you are of them.

In the same manner, I would encourage the girls about not having sex. Now remember, I started talking to them while they were young. I told them how I always thought it was fun to be different and to not have sex with a boy when I went out with him. Now I believe you will have a difficult time doing this with your children if they don't feel good about themselves. If they

72

don't have high self-esteem, feel positive and secure, they won't ever want to be different. They won't have the courage to stand up for what they know is right. All of these things work hand in hand. You can't do one without the other. You have got to build up the child's self-esteem, know their friends, encourage them with their goals and praise and encourage them if you don't want them to succumb to peer pressure.

When my children were little, they would tell me about the classmate who tried drinking, drugs or sex. I would always give my sympathy for the child. Again, it was my way of "planting seeds." I would say how sorry I felt for that child. I would ask my daughter if she knew of problems that child was going through as to possibly why they would think it necessary to give in to temptation to do these things. I would ask if she or he were getting enough attention at home. Did she know if the parents were having troubles in the home? Maybe his schoolwork was falling below average. I would always try to discuss with my daughter why she thought this child had to turn to drugs, drinking or wanting to give or get sex from someone to make him or her feel better. Instead of ignoring my little one's comments or, rather than get mad or upset about the other child, I would try to use this tragedy to teach my child something. Remember my purpose is to keep focused on using everything I could so my child would grow up not being weakened to give into temptation. What I was hoping is that when my child would be tempted she would think, 'Hey, why do I need this? I'm not having any troubles. My mom loves me. I'm a good person'.

If your children have established their goals at a young age then they will think about this too, when they're tempted to forget about the values and morals they have been taught. It makes sense that he or she will think 'Gee, if I take this drug, it might ruin my mind, and I won't be able to be a doctor or lawyer.' Goal setting is so important to the child. Life is going to tempt him and throw him around. If the children don't have a goal or plan, they will easily go the direction of their peers. When the goal is made, the child makes the commitment. Then it is our job, as parents, to mold and encourage those goals. Encourage the child to never compromise. Don't follow the crowd. It's important to the child that he can come to the home for a refuge and encouragement after he has been standing firm against peer pressure and temptations.

I want to have my child be able to tell me she said 'no,' and she knows I say 'no' to people when they ask me to participate too. I don't lecture my friends about drinking or drugs, but I am strong and don't sway to their offers. I would tell my daughters about all my experiences when I was on a date or in a group and people wanted me to participate in drugs, drinking or sex. I would let them know I said, "No" too and I'd often share with them the other people's response when I turned down their offer of temptation. It was practically always a response like, "Gee, I wish I didn't drink." Or as my best friend would say, "Don't offer Ginger a drink. She's crazy enough without it."

We want our kids to be leaders. Leaders are the ones who don't follow the crowd. Leaders are people who aren't afraid to be different. Leaders take risks. We should encourage our children to participate in as many activities as possible. This will get them involved. They will be building self-confidence and they will become little leaders. When summer comes, my girls were often asked to go to various camps. When they were a little younger, they wouldn't want to go. They thought they wanted to stay home and play with their friends. I wanted to give them the experience. I didn't want them sitting around the house with nothing to do. I wanted them to be with positive friends and young counselors. Still, I didn't want to be the meanie. I wanted this to be something they wanted to do. Therefore, if my daughter didn't want to go too readily, I came up with this agreement. If she would sign up for this week of camp, she could call me on the second day (or actually at any time), and I

74

promised that I would go get her and bring her home. Sure, it would have been a long drive and a real inconvenience for me. It could have been two, three or five hours away. But I agreed and promised her. I have to tell you that with all three girls and with the very many camps and trips they have taken, I NEVER had to go get them. In fact, it is very much the opposite. They would always call me to check in, and when I asked them how things were going, the answers were always that they were having a great time. I want you to know that my kids never knew my strategy. I don't tell them all my secrets of child raising. I just wanted them to know their happiness was the most important thing to me. I wanted them to feel absolutely confident that mom would always pick them up and bring them home if they weren't having a good time. If I didn't make them feel this way they would have gone off to all these camps kicking and screaming - mad at me - and definitely wouldn't have begun the week away from home with a positive attitude and they wouldn't have allowed themselves to have a good time and they would have called me on that second day to pick them up as they would have thought they were miserable. But because I had reassured them I loved them and only wanted them to be happy, they relaxed and went to the event and always actually had the best time of their lives. These opportunities give your child a chance to be away from home on some exciting venture and still be very supervised. They can do some wild and crazy things, but nothing illegal. Hopefully, they are associating with friends whose parents care as you and are making an effort to send their child on this special outing. These trips away from home will make your child feel better about himself and helps him grow into a leader. This will keep your child strong around peer pressure as it is just another way to help them feel good about themselves and they will have strength to stand up against wrong and hopefully make the right decisions.

If your child comes home and tells you about kids that cut classes and asked her or him to go along with them, listen to your child. Turn off the television and listen. Be so proud of your child for being strong. Remind him or her that was such a wise decision. All it would do is put them behind in their studies and it would be difficult to make up the assignment. Suggest that those kids probably don't have the high goals your child has and will probably never make it to college or at least to graduation. Feel sorry for the other kids. Be proud of your child. You are, once again, "planting your seeds." Maybe this would be a good time to say to your child, "I am so proud of you for being strong. Do you think you could get your homework done early, and we could go to the movie?" You can do that on a school night. These are things you can do as a single parent. You have the flexibility to do what you want. I would reinforce in your child that he did right, and you are proud of him. As the single parent, you have the time to listen and do things on the spur of the moment. You don't have to worry about being home to cook dinner or watch T.V. with your spouse.

When your child tells you about an incident that happened when a friend of his was hurt or picked on by all the other kids, and he stood up for that person, listen to him. Maybe it wasn't him who stood up for the other person, but he saw someone else stand up for that person. After you have listened, please praise and make a big deal out of how difficult it is to stand up for someone when everyone else is around. Remind him that he will some day be rewarded because some thing good will come to him in return from God. Tell him about how much character he has to stand up for what he thought was right. Let him hear you tell others how proud you are of his good act. This will continue to let him know that it is rewarding to stand up for what is right, instead of going along the wrong way with his peers.

Life isn't easy. If you are a single parent, you are evidence that life is very tough. You may feel life is difficult because you are a single parent. However, if this is your only concern, you are probably a lot better off than others. Wouldn't it be worse to be stuck in a terrifying or miserable marriage? Wouldn't the worst thing to happen to you be to lose your health? Aren't you fortunate you have a job? We aren't the only ones who think life isn't easy. Tough times seem to come to everyone in one way or another. If this remains true then it will probably be a fact that our children's life won't be easy either. We need to help prepare them to be strong. If we are going to equip our children to have courage, we need to start when they are young. You don't teach them to be strong by being strict, mean and giving them too many chores and responsibilities. I add this in right here because I think many people think we have to be mean to the child to make them tough. Being mean doesn't make them tough -- it makes them rebel and run, very quickly, to peer pressure. Of course, being mean could be interpreted in different ways. However, being mean is to give rules and orders without giving time to the child. Being mean is to deny the child the respect of listening, understanding, sacrificing and loving. If you don't have an equal balance you will know because your child will tell you "You are mean." As I have said before, I am a strict parent, but my girls have never called me a "Meanie."

How we prepare our child to be strong can't be explained in simple words. When I was only a very innocent 28 year old preacher's daughter, with no education and no confidence, I was left with two little girls. I was left with no money and I had to go on welfare. I survived. Everyone seemed amazed as to how I did it. I still can't put my finger on exactly why I came out of the situation positive and happy. I just have always said it had to be something my parents did. They must have instilled in me love, security and a will to never give up. I believed that something better would come in the future. I just had to keep believing and pressing forward.

It does seem quite clear that in order to survive in a successful way, in this world, we need to have self-control. Look at our adult lives. We have to be disciplined. Sometimes, this can be very painful. Our children need to know that they won't always be the ones to win. Even though they work very hard, they might not get the best grade on a school paper. Even though they practice an hour every day, they might make a mistake at their musical recital. They might have been the best basketball or soccer player last year, but maybe this year there will somebody better. Kids who are the good kids, -- who don't cheat, drink or take drugs -- do not always win. It's the same as with adults. From the outside, it doesn't always look like the good guy wins. Kids are not always going to win. This is where you can help them be strong. Let them know what they have learned from their hard work and discipline. Let them know they must keep up the hard work and practice because it will pay off later. The payoff might come next week on the test paper, or it might not happen until they get out into the world and on their own. Let the children know they must do the best they can in everything. The best for the children isn't always that they are number one in school -- it's that they are trying to do what is right. The advice we should give our children is that they know how to discipline themselves and have self-control so they will be better adults and make wise choices when they are grown.

As a single parent, you will have so much more time to listen and encourage your child than when you have a spouse in the house. Don't' feel sorry for yourself that you, "don't have anyone to love and take care of you." Just remember that you have a chance to mold and develop a beautiful character. You can't mold a spouse. This child gives you a chance to really do something good for all of America. If more parents could give the time you have to their child, there is no doubt that we would have a better society in the future. I look at it this way; I might not have turned out to be a financial genius. However, I have done better. I have had an affect on three girls, who, in turn, are contributing to the future of America. Because they are loved, educated and confident, they will turn around and bring better little people into the world. I would go through all the financial

78

sacrifices again as long as I could contribute these girls to make a better American society. Just think, if you are struggling monetarily or with romance and you don't put your children first, you won't have much of a success track when your life is over. Wouldn't it be a wonderful idea to give it your all for the kids? Then you will always be remembered as being such a good parent. That would be at least one great compliment they can say about you when you have left this world.

Don't forget, you can't expect to help your child through peer pressure if you wait until he or she is in the seventh grade. You must begin at birth.

SUGGESTIONS ABOUT WHAT TO SAY ABOUT THE "EX."

This chapter should be short. We don't want to talk too much about the "Ex," do we now? However, we can even find the positive in the "Ex." I used to say to friends, when I was defending my mistakes in marriage, "I really shouldn't have married him." Tami heard me say that one time. Later, she confronted me, "Mother how can you say that marrying dad was a mistake? You got me out of that relationship. Do you regret having me?" She was really broken-hearted because of what she had heard me say. She made me think. I apologized to her. I'm sure that you will agree that even out of the mistakes and a broken marriage you gained a wonderful blessing -- your children. I know that I would go through that rough marriage and shameful divorce again, if I could just have my girls. We can always find the positive. We can live the positive. Let's just concentrate on those children. Let's teach them how to be positive, happy little people.

When my first husband deserted me, at the age of 28, I seemed very much aware of the fact that this occasion could turn the girls bitter against all men. One always hears that some girl has a difficult time trusting men because of what her dad did. And I have met men who don't care to treat women nicely because they say they hate their mothers. I didn't want my girls to be bitter or hate anyone. I knew that if they had these feelings inside them, they would grow up with a real handicap. If they would look at men negatively or without trust, they might pass up love and a lot of happiness. I wanted them to get all the love and security they could out of this world.

On that memorable day, I decided to never talk bad about Terri and Traci's dad. I tried to not complain in front of them. It was my main objective to be happy around the girls. If I really

81

needed to bare my soul and cry, I would do it when they weren't around. When they asked about their daddy, I always spoke respectful of him. I would remind them that, "Daddy loves you very much. He was just sick, so he left." It just doesn't seem fair that a little child loses a father, which in itself is very traumatic, and then that child has to listen to mother moan and complain. I couldn't bring dad back. But I could concentrate on giving the girls a good life; that would begin with the girls not seeing bitterness in me.

I'll never forget that first Christmas, when I had to go buy that six foot Christmas tree all by myself. I was determined that I would make this Christmas like every other one. We would once again have the six foot tree. This tree had to be carried up four flights of stairs. I did it. I even got it standing in the stand straight. I am not a very physical person, and had always depended on my husband to do these types of things. However, it was up! I must admit that while I was struggling with that heavy tree, I wanted to just cry, but I kept reminding myself that wouldn't do any good. The girls might feel sorry for me and begin to hate men -- that could be the beginning of their anger. I wasn't going to be the cause of their hatred for men. After we got the tree all decorated, I told the girls I would make sure they could have every thing they had ever had, even though we didn't have a daddy.

So often a child hears a parent say, "We can't do that because we don't have enough money. Your mom takes all my money," or, "Your daddy doesn't give us enough money." I decided I would never blame the fact that we didn't have enough money on my girls' dad. Those kinds of comments are just bitter words. It took too much energy for me to be angry. I'd rather use my energy to be happy and get out there and try to make my own money. Whenever we didn't have enough money to go to a movie or out to eat, I would just say, "Oh, let's not go see that movie tonight. Let's take a picnic and go to the beach. Next week, we can go to the movie."

When you are around people who complain so much about someone, don't you wonder what the true story is? Don't you think, 'there are two sides of the story'? Don't you get irritated being around someone who is always saying the same negative things, over and over? Don't you get tired of being around men who are always down on women? Don't you always get tired of listening to women who are bitter about men? Well, can't you realize that is exactly the way your children will feel about you if you are always talking bad about their dad or mom? After all, it is their mom or dad. After my second divorce, when Tami returned to me after being with her dad, I was curious; I wondered if he was happy and how he was doing. I once asked Tami, "How is dad? Does he have a girlfriend?" She was a pretty sharp little eight year old and she said, "Mother, dad doesn't ask about you so I don't think you should ask about him." That remark hit me bluntly and I knew I wasn't to put her in the middle, causing her to tell things she felt uncomfortable about telling and maybe even thinking she would have to lie some day to make me feel good. I quickly learned to not ask questions about her dad and his lifestyle.

It appeared obvious to me that if I was as nice as I could be, and if I tried to be the best parent possible, my children would think I was a great person. They'd come to their own conclusion about their dad. Even if I bent their ears, always talking bad about their father, they would make up their own minds when they got older. I wanted them to think the best of me. I decided not to be a bitter person. I would just work on being the best mother possible.

It's really unfair to put the child in the middle of situations with you and your spouse. Soon after I left Tami's dad, she went to visit him. On her way out the door, I said, "Please ask Daddy to give you my child support check." Later, Stanley told me one of the best things he ever had said, "Gin, don't put Tamalani in the middle of our problems. If you want something, ask me directly." I listened to that, and did what he suggested. Since I moved out, my children have never seen a fight between my "ex" and me. It's not necessary to discuss things in front of the children.

When my brother was getting divorced, his wife used to really use the kids to hurt him. She wouldn't let them visit him like he wanted. He loved his kids. He had done some wrong things during his divorce, and his "ex" was very bitter. He soon recognized this and apologized to her. She still kept the kids from him. It hurt him very much. I suggested to Skip one day that he just tell his children how much he loved them. They really knew that and loved him too. I advised him that he tell his girls how very difficult it seems to be for their mother to let them visit him. He should make sure they knew how to reach him. Whenever they wanted and could get their mom to let them, he'd drop whatever he was doing in a flash to come pick them up. Since he lived about 100 miles away, he should write them often and call them when he could. He could always remind them he is waiting to hear from them. My suggestions were made because all these visitation problems were putting the girls in the middle. Nothing was really being accomplished; everyone was just fighting -- it's not good for the kids. I bet Skip that if he lay back and quit fighting with his "ex" for visitations, she'd soon get real tired and beg him to come take them away so she could have a free day or weekend. I'm not sure what Skip decided to do, but I hope he will think of the kids first and make a terrible divorce situation as easy as possible for them.

Don't be so angry with your "ex" that you are going to take the kids that certain day for visitation, no matter what, without thinking of the children. Think of what is best for the children; swallow your pride. If the child would rather stay home with the other parent because they have been invited to a friend's birthday party - work around it. If asking to see your child makes your "ex" put the child in the middle and in an uncomfortable position, possibly even having to lie to you, and making them fight with the other parent, then back down. Tell your child you so badly want to see them, but you see it is causing trouble and tension in the house. Tell them you want them, but you will wait until things are more comfortable and for them to call as soon as they are ready and you will come running. If that child doesn't call soon, keep calling and writing sweet little notes, but try not to make them uncomfortable with fighting in their present home.

The other day, I was sitting at a girls' softball game. A ball narrowly missed hitting a father of one of the girls. His "ex" was sitting near me. Everyone gasped, except this woman. She said, in front of her youngest daughter, "It should have hit him." What a nasty thing to say in front of your daughter about her daddy. The little eight-year-old loved her father. I could tell; they were always playing. The daughter must have hurt inside to know that anyone would say that about her dad. Did that mother think she was impressing the rest of us on the bleachers? It didn't impress me. I then realized why she had snotty girls. Her older girls were causing her big disappointments and embarrassments. They were projecting the same attitude the mother had shown them over the years. Did I mention that this same dad is paying for the house in which the mother and children are living? It just doesn't seem right to be so nasty to someone off whom you are living. If you dislike him so much, why don't you cut all financial ties?

Remember that the most important consideration is the well being of your children. Always ask yourself what's best for the kids. Get back at your spouse some other way. How about trying to make more money than him or her? How about finding someone sweeter than him or her to love? A sweeter person will more readily be attracted to you if you aren't always bashing your "ex." When your children get older and discover exactly what your "ex" did to you, they'll know you're the better person. I guarantee this. It happened to me. I get so much sympathy from my girls, now that I'm older. I love it!

YOU SHOULD TALK ABOUT SEX

Do you want your child to have sex at 13, 14 or 16 years of age? I don't think so. As soon as your baby is born, it is time to think about what you are going to do to help your child forego a temptation that is very normal to all humans and animals. It's very normal to want to have sex at any time and with anyone. It's our morals, values, goals and self-esteem that guide us and help us make wise decisions. I would probably want to have sex with anyone, at any time, if I hadn't been taught these important aspects of life. Just why is it kids want to have sex? Can you remember how it was when you were a kid? Let's think about it.

If you are a woman, do you remember the curiosity that drove you to look at other girls, when you took showers or when they spent the night? Do you remember how you searched your mind, wondering if you had ever seen a boy nude or even a picture of a nude boy? Boys begin to look at each other in the bathrooms. Remember how you were so anxious to see how you developed? You would worry that you wouldn't be big enough. Both boys and girls began to realize it felt good to touch their bodies. Do you remember then when a little boy or girl said something nice to us, how our heart began to pound? How can you forget that first little peck kiss? You thought it was just your heart pounding. It was blood pounding, and we all know that blood just doesn't pound in our hearts. We must not forget that everyone -- all boys and girls, including us, had these normal feelings. We still have these feelings.

What we did with our feelings depended on the values we had been taught. However, we could have been taught all the best of values in the world, but if we didn't have something inside of us, we would just ignore those values. That something inside of us is how we perceive ourselves. Let's go back again and think of our pre-teen and teen years. You can be honest with yourself. No one can read your mind. You will be admitting only to your self those things you did. Now, I would like to ask, do you care if your child does what you did? If you were a boy and did things with girls, do you want your daughter to do those things with boys? Do you want your son to treat girls like you treated them? Did you not give them as much respect as you should have because maybe you weren't actually told how to treat girls? If you were a girl, do you admit to doing some things, although maybe not real bad, but you wish your daughter would know that she doesn't have to do the same? Well, let's talk about it.

What do you think would have made you respond differently to those normal sexual situations? Could it have been, perhaps, no one talked to you about these feelings? Very probably, you were dying inside to ask questions of someone older -- someone who had experienced these same feelings, but you didn't know whom to ask for fear of embarrassment or lectures. Possibly, you could discuss these new feelings with an older person, but then you had another problem -- you still couldn't control your responses. I want to tell you how I handled sex with my girls. They seem to have come through those stages perfectly fine. They didn't "have to" get married. They had decided that they wanted to be virgins for their husbands so they did all they could to resist temptation. They felt comfortable talking to me about the temptations; I always understood because remember, I was single too (as you are) and I had to resist the same temptations. The older ones seem to have a good sex life with their husbands, so we'll see. . . When my first husband deserted me, Terri and Traci were six and two years old. My husband and I had a great sex life. He had taught me everything. He was very open and taught me to enjoy our intimacy. I was going to miss the sex because he was gone. Nevertheless, the big thought that came to me was that I would never wanted the girls to grow up frigid or not trusting men because of what their dad had done to me. I had heard so often that many women don't enjoy sex because of something that happened to them when they were little girls. I made a conscious decision to make men and sex a happy subject. I thought of the day when my daughters would be married and I didn't want anything that I had taught them, to have a negative effect on their marriage -- including that special time of intimacy. I determined to make the subject an open matter. I would be free to talk about how enjoyable it was to share sex. I would make it a fun topic and try to make them comfortable. As well, I would do my best to instill my morals within their little hearts and minds. As the single parent, you, too, can teach your values. You won't have a conflict that you might have had, should you disagree with a spouse's values and moral.

It appeared clear that I shouldn't give Terri and Traci the impression that men were bad. I thought my husband was crazy to leave me, but I didn't want to be fatalistic with the girls. This wasn't an issue of trying to win with my kids -- whether I was the good guy or dad was the bad guy. The issue now is how I wanted my children to develop. I tried to never talk negative about any man. It was important that I never said, "Oh, all men are like that." I didn't say anything about "All men." If I shared a conversation with the girls about something a man had done -- that we thought was inappropriate, I would say, simply, "That's too bad he (that one man) had to say or do that." I never categorized all men. I never made fun of men or "man bashed." If someone I knew or a comedian on T.V. made fun of men, I didn't roar with laughter. I tried to ignore it. There are definite traits that seem to run with the sexes. Men have just as many reasons to bash women, but it just didn't seem good for my girls, or even me, if I started being negative and making fun of men. First of all, we do have to admit that there are good men as well as there are good women, in spite of what has happened to us. And now the issue is not to get back at men or women because of what we have gone through, but to raise future children who will be happy, secure, financially stable and well adjusted. A real advantage of being the single parent is that you can make up your mind on what to say, in front of your children, about men and women. In most married families, that I have observed, at least one of the parents always thinks he or she has to be the comedian and put down the other gender. We see this on television all the time. If you decide as the single parent that you are not going to do this, then you don't have to worry about a spouse always refuting you in front of the kids. What good are a few laughs for your own ego, if you are affecting the children to be negative, bitter people of the future? I realized that I could control my reactions about men. I knew I didn't have a husband to influence the girls. Regardless, I was aware that the girls would be somewhat influenced by other children and television. I couldn't do much about what other children said. However, I could control the television. I'm quite liberal with what the girls watch on T.V. Nevertheless, I had to only watch one program of Married With Children and The Simpsons to know that what they are putting into our children's minds is not healthy. Perhaps adults can watch the way moms and dads are severely made fun of and not be adversely affected. Still, I knew that Terri, Traci and Tami were in the growing stages. I wanted to help the future society be better. Putting people down can't help make this a better world. I wouldn't let my children watch a program that criticized different races. I would refuse to let them watch a program the put down America. These are all things that are causing riots and affecting the future of America. Well, if I think the American family is the most important institution, I wanted to do my part to improve the situation. I couldn't change America, but I could start in my home, with my own girls.

When children are very little, there isn't a lot of talk about sex. However, you may see them play or touch themselves. That's normal. We touch ourselves too. We just do it when no one is looking. When Terri began to ask about where babies came from, I was very honest. At first, I was apprehensive about how I'd handle this. I remember the first serious answer I gave her "Babies come from the mother's tummy." I sat there

90

sweating, wondering what I'd answer to her next question. She didn't ask the next question at that time. Later, as she would ask another question, I would just answer what she asked. There were times, as she got older, that I remembered my own curiosity at her age, and I would try to carry on the conversation to a little deeper depth. For example, when Terri was six, she asked me an awkward question; she asked what men look like in their private area. Terri was a very mature six-year-old. She had skipped two grades and was in third grade, so she was asking a question that an eight-year-old might ask. I didn't immediately know how to answer her. I just knew I had to answer every question she asked, if I wanted to keep the communication open between the two of us. I wanted her to always feel free to ask me anything, instead of going to her friends. I began, "Oh, I realize why you are asking that question. You have never even seen a little brother, a baby boy or even remember having a glance at your dad. I'll see if I can find a picture for you." Now none of this was real easy for me. I was young and had grown up quite innocent. However, as always, I wanted to put my feelings aside and do all that was possible to help this child grow up in the best way. If I laughed, criticized or didn't give Terri an adequate answer, she would go get her answers elsewhere. Our communication with regard to sex could end right here. The first place I began to look for pictures was in my medical book -- those were sketches or diagrams showing how the penis functions. It would give a sufficient answer for medical questions, but I knew very well Terri was just curious as to what a real penis looked like. I had no pictures at home. I decided to embarrass myself and go to the drug store to purchase a *Playgirl* Magazine. I took it home very sheepishly. I just wasn't into looking at men's nude pictures, but this was for my daughter. I sat Terri down next to me on the couch and told her, "I understand why you are curious. I would be to. So, I went and bought a magazine that has pictures of men in it. I will show you the picture. After you are finished looking, I will throw the magazine away, as mom doesn't have any reason to hang on to it." She looked at it. It took about 15 seconds and that was that! I was keeping the communication open. I did it with good taste. I let her know she could ask me questions about sex. By the way, now we always get a big laugh because of the way I handled this; but it worked. Now it seems very funny and probably would shock some people.

The next few years, children are basically learning how babies are made. They learn a little more in school each year. I would continue discussions with them. That was easy. As they continued to grow, there were times when I would jokingly say things like, "Gee, that was fun to go to the amusement park this Sunday afternoon. If I was still married to dad I would be wanting to make love." They would always say "Mom!" I would enjoy embarrassing them in this simple way, just to let them know sex is a subject that can be discussed. I would laugh them off and say "Well, that's normal between married people. You think we're taking a nap. Hmm." That's all the longer the conversation would take. I just wanted to 'plant my seeds' that sex was nice.

I took advantage of every opportunity that came into our lives to 'plant those seeds' and to protect the girls. In the teen years, I enjoyed the popular music station as much as the girls. Naturally, there are songs that come on that don't have very tasteful words. They talk a lot about sex. I would use that time to share with the kids, whoever was in the car. I would remind them "That's not a nice song. Now, why do they have to talk like that? The tune is so nice. They don't have to use that kind of language." Instead of screaming to change the radio station, I would make it a learning time. Most of the songs (I didn't listen to hard rock) are very pretty, with nice love meanings. When a sweet song came on I would acknowledge it by saying "That's a pretty song." I complimented the good ones, so that I wasn't known as just a nag, complaining about all the songs that kids like to listen to. Remember, my purpose was to keep the communication open between the teenagers and me. However, when a nasty song came on, I was then entitled to make my teaching comments. Many times I have said, "That's a beautiful song for lovers. It's for married people. You need to wait to listen or sing this song until you are married." I was trying to put the songs that referred to having sex in perspective. I would remind them that those sex songs are fine when you are married. They were learning values of when sex is right and when it is not right. I was not excluding myself from their conversation by refusing to let them listen to the popular radio station. It just doesn't work to forbid your children to listen to all the music that is on the air. They are going to hear it at school, when kids sing them. They'll hear it at school concerts. They'll hear it when they ride in other kids' cars and when they visit in other kids' homes. It's up to you to teach your child the proper values. Through the same discussions, you can teach your child about sex.

Our main purpose in discussing sex with our children is to give them values. We want them to have good sex lives. We want them to know when they should have sex. Quicker than we realize, our kids are in the age bracket where they are beginning to have the urge to have sex. Their friends are having sex. Think back about why you, as a little girl, found it difficult to say "no" to the boy. Were you afraid he wouldn't like you anymore? We want to make certain that our little girl feels good enough about herself that she doesn't have to fear losing a boy because she did what she thought was right. The only way this will happen is if they have good self-esteem. Hopefully, they have been developing this high self-esteem all their lives. If your daughter knows she has a lot of good things going for her, she will be able to say no to sex and know that boys will like her for other reasons. When she is in that tempting situation, she will be able to think about what she has going for her in her life. She will realize that this is an opportunity for her to stand on her own.

She will know she can survive. In the long run, she will feel better about herself.

Your daughter needs to be prepared for that first time when she has the strong urge to have sex. I remember when Traci was 14 years old and she told me, "Mom, I think I'm in love. But don't worry mother, I won't have sex." Later that day, I had a phone conversation with her older sister, who was away at college. I said to Terri, "Traci says she's in love, but she promises not to have sex." Terri said, "Mother, you need to prepare her about how she will handle it, when she does get that urge." That sounded like good advice. When I saw Traci later, I asked to talk to her, "Traci, mom, is so proud of you that you don't ever plan to have sex. However, I want to tell you that no matter how strong you feel, some day, you will be passionately kissing and the desire to have sex will be very forceful. You need to prepare now about how you will handle it when the moment arrives, or you won't be able to prevent it. It is very difficult to stop when you get into that situation." I was doing three things with this conversation. I was bragging to her about how pleased I was that she wasn't going to have sex. Also, I was keeping the doors open by letting her know that I understood sex and that it was a good, strong feeling that was normal. Then, I went on to talk about the repercussions of having sex at an early age and before marriage. I didn't want to make this conversation a lecture, so I said things as quickly and briefly as I could. I determined I would skip over the part about sex before marriage being adultery. Traci was a good Christian girl and in church she had heard that sermon many times. I would go on to the immediate results of having sex too soon even as the world looks on it. I told her that the sex drive seems to be stronger in men (I don't think I really agree with that, but I wanted her to know it was very strong). I told her that probably all boys and men will want sex, even if they know it's wrong. I feel that it is up to we girls, to control the situation. I informed her that men almost always wanted sex from me too. I was telling her I had to handle

94

the same situations she had to face. I, in turn, let her know I liked sex, but we had to think with our mind and not our heart. I told Traci that I don't think it's fair for a girl to tease and lead a guy on and then just expect him to stop when we suddenly come to a panic situation and say, "please stop." It's rough on the guy. It's seems only courteous to not give the guy the impression you are going to go "all the way." If you are heavily petting and saying things, what can you expect the guy to think? Nevertheless, there will come the time when you yourself don't want to stop. You must get prepared. You must think about how you will feel the next day. It is my concern that so often it seems that if a girl has sex for the first time, she thinks she's in love with the boy. Suddenly she will have shared the most special moment of intimacy that could never belong to anyone else. Again she will think she is in love and, of course, she will be absolutely certain that the boy loves her. She will want only him and won't even want to date anyone else. She will want to marry this guy. After all they have a special relationship already. Well, it just makes common sense that at 14 or 15 years of age no one can know that this is the man with whom she wants to spend the rest of her life. Clearly, it seems like this is one of the reasons there are so many divorces. People don't wait long enough and date enough to make sure they have the right person. When a person has sex, that it is such a good intimate feeling that they no longer think logically. I reminded Traci that she doesn't want to be a divorce statistic. She wants to go to college and date and travel and have lots of fun before she settles down. I pointed out that the kind of mate a person wants at 18 is very often not the same type of person one wants at 25. People are still maturing becoming more educated and our ideas are just beginning to develop. In addition, I reminded her that if she did succumb to temptation, she might feel guilty and be mad at herself because she really didn't want to, but at that one moment couldn't resist the temptation. There is also the reason to not have sex with the boy because he might talk to his buddies. He might only tell one person, but this is a big thing to guys, and they might all just tell one other friend.

Sex is just something everyone wants to tell someone else that so and so has done it. Would she want all the guys talking about her? Over the years, I had heard guys say that they want sex, so they would get it from whomever they could, but they didn't want to marry that girl who had been passed around. Someday, I told her, there will be the right man out there who will want that girl who waited for him. Lastly, I spoke about being different. I knew Traci had high self-esteem up to this point. It was easy for me to remind her how beautiful she was. She was very smart. She was athletic. She had high values. A lot of guys would want a girl like her. "Traci, BE DIFFERENT," I told her. Have the boys want you because you are different. Give them a challenge. Have them like you for some quality other than sex.

It's ironic, but Tami had exactly the same experience at the age of 14, when she was visiting her dad one summer. She called me and said, "Mother, I'm in love. Don't worry, though, I've made up my mind. I'll never have sex." Even though it had been about nine years since I had the discussion with Traci, I remembered what Terri had advised me at that time. I said to Tami at that late hour of 3:30 a.m., on the telephone "Tami, we need to talk for a few minutes." I then gave her the same short praise and warning conversation that I had given to Traci nine years previously. I simply cautioned her that some day she is going to have such a strong urge to have sex that she needs to prepare now for how she is going to handle it so she won't give in to temptations and have regrets.

It's necessary that I say something for you parents of boys with regard to sex. It's obvious that I have never experienced raising boys. However, I might know how they treat girls, pertaining to sex, even more than you as parents of boys. I know specifically what they say and do to girls. Also, because, I like kids, I have very bluntly talked to boys, particularly those who were dates and boyfriends of my girls. While raising my girls, I have sat on the bleachers with many parents of boys. It never seems that parents are too concerned about boys and how they treat girls with regard to sex. The most I think I have ever heard a parent of a boy say, "I tell him to take protection." To me, that seems so minor when I think of everything else that is involved with sex. Protection is easy to get. It takes no work, no brains, no money, least of all, no values. Please help teach our future generation values and how to be thoughtful of each other. Don't lecture you sons. Let them know you have the same sex urges. Tell them how they can handle them and fight them off. Tell them the same things that I tell the girls. They have their whole life in front of them. They might think they are in love if the sex is so good (and it has been said, it doesn't take much sex for a guy to think it was good, right?). Perhaps your sons sexual experience might have him, not have the pleasure of dating many girls, going to college and traveling before he makes that serious decision of a commitment. The girl he chooses to make love with will positively think she is in love with your son and she will do everything in her power to try to get your son to marry her. Don't you want you son to finish college, travel and date several girls to make sure he marries the right one so that he, too, won't end up a divorce statistic? Sure you do! Remind them of the obligations of house payments, bills and, no doubt, the wife will want to have kids and the husbands have to face this additional tremendous responsibility. It's manifested from the divorce rate that it's these very people who marry young who, all of a sudden hit an age of 30 or 40, and they get tired of the responsibility. Life isn't fun anymore! They begin to think they missed out on something. They got married at such a young age and only dated one or two people. They didn't go away to college or perhaps they regret they didn't just travel with their friends and have freedom before they decided to settle down. Now all they seem to have are regrets and little children who are very demanding and there is always one bill after another to be paid. One begins to have extra-marital affairs. Or one just wants out, as there seems to be too much pressure; whereas couples that have waited longer to marry are more settled in their financial situation. They

97

know what it's like on the other side. They know the 'grass isn't always greener.' They have got the freedom out of their system and they are ready to choose the person that will be just right for them and settle down. They are matured and ready for responsibility and raising children.

When Tami was in the 11th or 12th grade, I had a boy at my house who was going to take Tami on a date. I happened to know that he had sex with another girl. Tami had told me. Actually he had told me himself a few months previously, when he wasn't dating Tami and had called to ask me for advice with his previous girlfriend. While he was sitting in my living room that night, I teasingly said, "Now you both have a good time. Don't have sex with Tami now, or I'll get you for rape." I was smiling and laughing, but I was hoping that when he got tempted, those thoughts of Tami's mom would flash through his mind. Also, it was my way of reminding him that I knew about his past, one-time experience. I was letting him date my daughter, but I expected the most consideration from him. I wasn't worried about Tami being tempted to have sex because she had her high goals. I did go on to say, "You know, I'm dating out there all the time. I have always said that if a guy just wouldn't come on to a girl so quickly. If he would not say anything about sex, it wouldn't take too long until a girl would want it and be all over the guy. You guys shouldn't let a girl think that sex is all you want. You should make it like a carrot dangling out there. You should go out with the girl because you like her personality. You should be considerate of the girl's feelings and how having sex might affect her whole life. When you marry there will be every night of the week to have sex and do it right" This guy is such a cute kid. As he left my door, he said, "Oh, I'll bring Tami home before that. I'm not going to rape her tonight. I'm going to keep that carrot dangling." We laughed. He got my point. We could talk. My plan was that if they ever got tempted, they could talk about it between themselves and laugh about something mom had said. I had another motive in mind. I didn't think Tami would really get serious with this boy because of things she had said, however I was very concerned about the boy and I was hoping that maybe I could 'plant a few seeds' in his mind that might help him with future relationships.

Now, it is true, perhaps, I could say these things with kids a lot more comfortably than some of you. It's because I love kids so very much and it just was easy for me to show it. It's also because I haven't forgotten how it was when I was their age. As a single parent, I could have these discussions and feel free to talk. I never could have talked like this if I had been married. It would even be embarrassing for me to talk to a big husky guy, like I did this date of Tami's, if I had a husband sitting next to me on the couch. Fathers of girls want to scare the guy and be tough. They could never talk lightly or even think about making a joke. Well, that's O.K. if that's what you want to do, but I bet my way worked better. There is no doubt that this guy wouldn't have been as free to listen, laugh and make his comment about keeping the carrot dangling if dad had been there. But, please parents of boys; do have open talks with your boys about girls and sex.

Continually, I planted my seeds. When I would see a girl on the news or in the community who got pregnant, I would say with all sincerity, "Isn't that too bad. Now maybe she'll think she has to marry the boy. That's going to ruin all her plans for college. She won't have the opportunity to travel and have fun before she faces the responsibilities of raising children." When Tami tells me about a girl at her high school having sex, I say, "Oh, that's too bad. Doesn't she know that soon everyone will know and talk about her? I wonder why she gave in to temptation. She must not have felt very good about herself." Once again, I use these sad, tragic stories to turn them around -- to make something positive for my child. I say, "Tami, mom is so proud of you that you will say no to sex. You know you have

99

so much more going for you than just sex. If you had sex you might think you are in love and want to marry the guy. You would miss out on all those fun years of college. Possibly you would never be able to be that Supreme Court judge you want to be. Everyone would be talking about you. Doesn't it feel good to be different from all the other girls at school who are giving sex out so easily? And you are so well liked. You are giving strength for others to say "no" to sex."

When you have good communication with your child, you're going to hear everything. Many things will shock you. But, would you rather hear about them or have the kids just talk amongst themselves? I have told you this example in a previous chapter, but I think it's worth repeating in case someone is just reading this chapter alone. I will never forget Tami's first year here in California. She was in eighth grade. I picked her up from school one day and she said, "Bobby, asked me to give him a blow job." Inside of me, I screamed, 'What?!!' My hands tightened around the steering wheel. Quickly, I thought, 'I'm glad she can tell me. I don't want to take this freedom to talk away from her. I guess these things are going on in the real world. I'll try to help her get through it.' I took a deep breath and said, "What did you answer him?" She said she didn't reply, as she didn't know what to say. I then told her that this is something all boys and men enjoy. I explained that they think we girls want to do it to them. I told her that even men who ask me out want me to do it to them. Therefore, she needs to know how to handle it. I said, "You don't have to get mad and slap the guy. It's up to you to control it. It's good if you can handle it with humor." That's about all we said. The next day, I picked Tami up after school, and she said, "Johnny asked me to F--- him." Wow! We don't use those words in our house. We don't even say 'stupid' or 'shut-up'. What was happening to my little girl's environment? Again, the blood pressure was rising and I took a deep breath and said, "What did you say?" Tami said, "I told him I'm waiting for somebody who was experienced." I snickered and said "Good for you. That was a good answer." I complimented her on putting this little eighth grader in his place without having to get nasty. Now, for the first moment I did think, 'I'm going to go to the principal and tell him what these kids are saying.' Then I wondered just what good would that do. It would definitely embarrass my daughter -- the new girl on campus. The principal can't change the way these kids have been raised. Tami is going to face this type of confrontation all her life. I better use this opportunity to guide her as to how to handle herself for now and in the future.

Not too long after this incident, Tami told me that at P.E. that day the girls had been lying around the tennis courts and they had talked. She was still just getting acquainted at this new school. She proceeded to tell me that this one girl in seventh grade was telling the rest that she had sex with this boy. WHAT? I was shocked! What would I do without the opportunity for deep breaths to relax? Once again, I quickly thought, 'I don't want my daughter hanging around her.' I went on to think, 'Now, I don't want to stop the communication here, so I better be careful what I say.' I asked, "Did the little girl say she liked it?" Tami said she didn't even think to ask her that question. I continued to think about how I would respond to what I had just heard. Instead of going off on this girl, whom I'm not responsible for, I would try to turn this example around to plant my seeds for my daughter. I said, "Oh, I was just curious as to whether she enjoyed it or not. You know that one of the biggest complaints older, married men have is that their wives are frigid and don't enjoy sex (Hey, I figure I can be as blunt as I want -- with style and class -- because these kids are hearing everything on the school grounds), and I can't help but think it's because the girl's first experience was perhaps in the back seat of a car or in a rushed and scared atmosphere. Also, boys can have a climax real fast and they feel good. It usually takes a girl or woman a little longer. Young boys don't know how to make the girl feel good. They haven't had a chance to learn. Girls have sex to make their boyfriends happy, but sooner or later they think sex is no big deal -- sex isn't really enjoyable, they have never had or even know what a climax is all about. Then as they get older, marry and are comfortable, they tell their husband they don't really enjoy sex. The husband has to always wonder what he did wrong and how he can get the wife excited so she will enjoy sex. I can't help but think that if the girl would have waited until she were older and married, by then the man would know how to treat the woman and make her feel satisfied. She would have had a great experience; then she would enjoy sex and she would always want it as much as her husband." That's all that was said. It sounds pretty forthright, but I determined that if Tami can be so direct by telling me what the kids are discussing at school, I should be just as explicit with what I teach her at home. I never again brought up these examples. I didn't keep throwing them into the conversation to remind Tami not to have sex. If I did that, she would regret the moment she ever told me anything. By the way, that day I asked Tami, "Do the other girls tell their mothers what you just told me?" She explicitly said, "No way! Their moms would have a fit." Would you rather have a fit and have your daughter not talk to you, or would you rather handle it in a way similar to what as I did?

During her senior year, Tami came home from school and told me about a senior boy who broke up with a senior girl. Both were nice kids and leaders. I acknowledged that the break up was too bad and asked what had happened that made them break up. Tami said that the boy wanted to have sex and the girl wouldn't give it to him. Instead of getting irritated with the boy (I knew that wouldn't help anything. He's really a nice boy. Tami liked him. It would irritate her if I talked bad about her friend), Instead, I bragged about the girl. I said, "Oh, I'm so proud of Sherry. Doesn't that make you feel good too, Tami? There is another popular girl (she was a cheerleader) who has the same high morals as you." That's all I had to say. I planted my seeds. As we drove away, I was thinking about Sherry, and I thought,

'You know, there are awards out there for the best athletes, the students who make Honor Roll, even at the end of the year there are awards for the best smile, but no one seems to be recognized for not succumbing to peer pressure.' I determined to let Sherry know I respected her. Of course, I would be tactful and let her know when no one else was around and not say too much to make her feel uncomfortable, but I knew that all the kids at school probably knew why they broke up and she needed to be acknowledged for standing up for what she knew was right. About a month later I had an opportunity to call her and I said, "Sherry, I just want to tell you that Tami told me why you broke up with Justin. I am sorry, but I want to tell you how proud I am of you for sticking to your values and desire to remain a virgin. There are so few out there, and I want you to know how much I admire you." She said, "Thank you," and I knew it was an unusual phone call. Still I wanted her to know that the good girls do get recognized. A few weeks later, I ran into her mother, whom I hardly knew. Her mother said, "Ginger, that was so nice of you to call Sherry. That came at a time when she really needed to hear a word of encouragement." I felt I had inspired another kid. I knew I had done a good deed. It's ironic that soon this boy began dating another sweet girl on campus. I couldn't resist asking Tami, "Will Carly give him sex"? She said, "No, She's just like Sherry." That was great. There are good kids out there. Our kids need to hear about them. This boy really likes the nice girls. He naturally has a desire for sex, but as long as the girls control the situation, everything stays on level ground. Always remember to emphasize the positive and skip over the negative. If you've been teaching your children values and self-esteem all their lives, they know what is right or wrong. They need to know they will be recognized and appreciated for being honorable.

Because I was a single mom and dating, like my teenagers, I knew that we were both going through the same enticement. Many times it was difficult for me to not invite my date into my house and my bedroom. However, I would always think of the example I had to be to my daughter. If I was telling her she could withstand temptation, then I knew I had to be the example. I don't want you to think I was so perfect and resisted all temptations -- I wasn't and didn't, even though I really tried. If you want to have your private times; then just do it with class. Don't do it in front of the child. If you have the attitude, 'It's my house and I can do what I want,' then you will be teaching your child a lesson that no one can resist the lure of sex. Why should your child think he should have morals, if mom or dad don't have any? On the other hand, if they are tempted and while they are passionately kissing they think, mom or dad is on a date trying not to have sex, so I can try to defy the temptation too.

If you don't want your children to have sex when they are teenagers, you need to start very early by encouraging them to participate in sports, music or some extracurricular activities that will keep them very busy. Yes, I have said that self-esteem is extremely important. These extra involvements will be helping that self-esteem. At the same time, these activities will be keeping your children so busy that they can't just hang around the house after school or in the summer. If your children have never played sports, you can't wait until they are about 12 or 13, and you are in fear of them being tempted for sex, and then you try to encourage them to play sports. It's very difficult, if not impossible, to come in at this late time in their life and qualify for the team. Not only that, your children won't have the confidence to even try out for the sporting event. If they have never played any sport, they will know that it is almost impossible to begin now. They won't even try. It is very embarrassing for a child of this age to not make the team. That is a severe rejection. It wouldn't be fair to your kid. You must begin when they are three or four. Sign those little tykes up for gymnastics, dance, soccer, whatever. Just get them into the habit of being involved. Always have them engrossed in something other than schoolwork. After a while, it's just accepted that they

104

are to decide what they want to do with regards to an extra activity. They will have that desire in them to get involved. They will have developed that competitive nature, or perhaps that nature to help by being a member of student council or the newspaper. Maybe they will have the character to just entertain with the music or dancing. It's a personality that you have helped create. You have done an excellent job, if your child wants to be a participant. Otherwise, your child will just grow into an insecure, couch potato with no drive or energy. They will have lots of idle time to be available to have or give sex. They won't feel good about themselves and think they have anything else to offer the opposite sex.

When Terri was six, I began in the summer months by taking her to the YWCA. Lessons are much cheaper there. At first, she took swimming lessons. She was very good, but she didn't seem to enjoy it; maybe because they thought she had real potential and wanted to groom her for the Olympics. She got exhausted swimming the full length of that Olympic size pool. The thought of her winning awards and maybe making the Olympics sounded good to me, the proud parent. However, I saw how much she didn't like it. I chose to let her drop out, with the idea we would try something else. She then took tennis, trampoline, sewing and just about everything available. She got into the habit of belonging to groups and activities. Later, when she got to sixth grade, she was ready to join the sports teams at school. She also became a cheerleader. She continued to play sports, be a cheerleader and sing in a girl's ensemble all through high school. Traci was the same. She started at about three years old, taking dance and gymnastics. She, too, went on to play volleyball and basketball in school every year, and be a cheerleader. Tami is an exact pattern of her sisters. She just couldn't go one semester without playing sports. The girls were so busy with games and practices after school that they hardly had time to see boys. Oh, they made time for dates, but they eliminated the possibility of idle time. They were so exhausted from the homework and the sweating; they had almost burned up all their energy for sex. Hopefully, you can see, that by starting early to involve your child you are giving him or her self-esteem. That self-esteem will give them confidence to know he or she doesn't have to give in to the desires of sex. When your child begins to be with the opposite sex he or she won't feel they have to impress their boyfriend or girlfriend with sex. Your child will be proud of his involvement in other activities. He will feel good about himself. It also, gives him something more to talk about when the kids are together. If kids can't talk about a sporting event or a school club, they will begin to talk about sex. I have personally noted that this happens in my case. There have been men whom I accepted a date with and enjoyed the first evening. We were able to get acquainted and find out a little about each other. However, as the dates went on, if the man didn't have any extra involvements to talk to me about, the conversation would sort of come to a lull. I could watch it coming. Because of a lack of something to talk about, the man would invariably bring up the topic of sex. By involving your child, he is getting so busy, that he doesn't have idle time to "hang around" and get tempted.

It takes a lot of time to take your children to these lessons and sporting events. Most of the time is when they are very young. Later, they will just stay after school. Actually, this will be good for you, the single parent. You won't be worrying at the office, while you have to stay at work until 5:00, about where your child is hanging around or who she has in the house. You will know she is in the school gym or on the sporting field. Should you ever think, 'This child takes too much of my time. I'm only a taxi driver,' just remember this is your investment for your future. If you don't take the time now, you will be spending many hours listening and helping them out of troubles all their life. This is the advantage of being a single parent. You will have lots more time to take your child to all of his endeavors. You won't have to worry about being home to cook dinner or fix something for your spouse. You can even use that hour while your child is at a practice to get caught up on some of your reading or letter writing. It is an excellent opportunity to get to visit and meet the parents of the other kids with whom your child is playing. You can help determine if this is the type of family you want your child to be involved with and - after practice or the meeting is over, you still don't have to go home to cook. You can stop at the fast food and pick up dinner, if you want. As the single parent, you can be helping your child grow into a more fully developed person and you don't have to rush home to your chores. No one will be waiting at home to ask where you have been. Use the opportunities as the single parent to talk about these personal matters and become closer acquainted with your child. Don't feel sorry for yourself.

YOU WANT TO HAVE A CLOSE FAMILY --
THOSE FAMILY TIES!

It might seem difficult to have a close family or even impossible to feel like a "family", since you are a single parent. You must know that it can be done. You are a family! You are a single parent family, and you are going to have as good as or better family situation than anyone you might know.

Studies have shown that family traditions are important to keeping the family together. It seems that children rely on that stability, as well as adults. Going through that divorce caused a lot of turmoil for your child. Perhaps there was a lot of confusion surrounding the children before you made the final decision to get divorced. No doubt, you're thinking that you will never be a real family again. Please don't let that thought enter your mind. You are a real family. In fact you're going to be happier now, simply because you are not living in that very unhappy relationship. You can make your children know they're in a complete family and they won't feel that they are missing out because they don't have the other parent in the house. When Traci was about five years old, we were moving into a new neighborhood. She told me what the neighbor boy said when he asked if we had a daddy and she told him we didn't. He said, "You're lucky. I wish I didn't have a daddy. I don't like mine." On the same hand, seventeen years later I heard the same kind of remark, when I told Tami's 15 year old friends that Tami didn't have a daddy living with us, three of the girls said how lucky she was because they didn't like their dads. One girl said, "I have two dads, and I wish I didn't have either." Another girl said, "Tami can have my dad." These were very sad comments. I didn't like to hear them, but I pass it on to you only so that you will realize you aren't in a terrible situation because you don't have a dad or mom in the house. You are actually envied, by not only kids, but also unhappily married couples. So. don't feel sorry for yourself. Twist this negative situation around and into a positive situation and realize you, alone, can make your family a close-knit family.

Research has shown that happy families enjoy traditions they have experienced over the years. These bring back memories of a happy childhood. Each family can make their own traditions. It's a good idea to think if there were any traditions your parents observed that bring pleasure to you when you think about them. Perhaps your dad would sit in front of the Christmas tree on Christmas morning and read the Christmas story out of the Bible. My dad did that, and even though I was so anxious to get to the presents, I remember so much that tradition of the family being together. When I had children, I decided that even though we didn't have a dad, I would read the Christmas story to the girls. It isn't so much who does it, but that you do it and that it be done every year. Perhaps you come from a divided or unhappy family and you can't remember any good traditions. Determine that you want to give your kids some good memories of things you did together. Maybe you can think of some ideas from what your friends did that you might have envied. Otherwise, maybe I can give you some suggestions and at least get your mind stimulated. These traditions will keep those family ties. You have to be consistent; but it's so much fun.

A great compliment came when Terri told me she wanted to have some traditions when she began her family. She told me how her husband had liked the fact that our family really made a big thing of holidays and birthdays. That made me realize that what I did to keep the family close was admired and could be done by the single parent. My son-in-law came from a great family, but apparently he wanted our types of celebrations for his little ones. Never think or say you can't do such and such because you don't have a husband or wife in the house. Don't sit around and wait for grandparents or aunts and uncles to establish your traditions. You begin planning them today.

110

So what if you are a single dad and you remember that every birthday your mother decorated a beautiful cake or perhaps baked a delicious smelling pie? You can go to the bakery and get one of the most exquisite and yummy cakes available. Besides, very possibly, if you were married, your wife probably wouldn't bake that cake these days anyway. Life is too busy. Very few modern mothers have the time to bake that cake. You just have to make a slight adjustment. Your child will never know the difference. He will just always remember that every year on his birthday, dad bought the most beautiful cake, to help celebrate.

Perhaps your father used to take you out into the woods to cut down a tree at Christmas time. That was such a good time for the kids. If you are the mother and feel you don't have the strength to cut down the big ole' tree, then you can adapt. In the cities, where you can't go out in the woods and chop down your own tree, they are many Christmas tree farms or a big Christmas tree lot, where you and the kids can walk up and down the aisle and choose the tree you want. The man will cut it down for you if it's growing or he'll bind it up for you to take home. That seems like great fun for your children. They will feel they have a part in picking out the tree, just as you did when you were a kid. Your child will never feel short-changed for not actually watching a dad cut the tree. Probably he will never even know the difference. At Christmas, I made sure we got the tree together.

Sometimes, it's difficult to capture that busy teenager, but it's just more fun to go with him or her. I baked cookies and made candy at Christmas. Because I had all girls, we were always counting the calories, and I'd think I shouldn't waste my time doing all that baking. However, I continued to do these things so I would be keeping the tradition that hopefully would mean something to them when they grew up. It was my part in keeping the family close. Instead of worrying that we would eat too many goodies, and rather than feel sorry that I no longer had a husband to eat my baking, I packaged these baked items and gave them to the girls' teachers or coaches. It's easy to get discouraged at times and want to stop a tradition, but you must not. Your child will appreciate those traditions much more than you realize. You are contributing to making your family have those close ties and good memories.

In our family we made all holidays and birthdays very special. I think it is so important for my girls since the other days of the weeks throughout the year were very hectic and filled with stress. The holidays made me slow down and do something special for the girls. It made them slow down and do something special for me; like enjoy and appreciate my efforts.

In all actuality, it is undoubtedly much easier to keep the family close together on the holidays then to make time to be together day after day. A family today isn't the way it was when our parents were growing up. There was no television, and families would sit around playing games and doing puzzles. There weren't as many sports and activities for children to be involved with in the 50's and even the 60's. When I was growing up, I had the opportunity to take swimming lessons in the summer, but that was about all that was readily available. I played volleyball and softball, but those games took place usually during the school day or immediately after school. While my girls played these same sports, they had hours and hours of practice. They were required to attend the different sport camps. When they played on the junior varsity teams, they were compelled to stay to cheer on the varsity team. Coaches are now demanding as much from girl's teams as boy's teams. It was very rare that Tami ever was able to leave the gym until 6:00 P.M., and many nights, particularly when the team played out of town, she didn't get home until 10:00 P.M. She would be all wound up, worn out and feel the pressure to get her homework done. It was a hectic life, but I would have much rather had her

112

participating in her sports than doing the opposite, be idle and possibly become involved in drugs, drinking and other troubles, like so many kids we knew. I just say all of this to let you know that I definitely know it is difficult to keep the family close; but it can be done. Even if your child stayed home every night, you might not be close, unless you put forth some effort.

I determined years ago that we would only have one T.V. in our home (except for a while when I had a little T.V. in the bathroom to watch the news in the mornings). It had come to my attention that so many of the girl's friends all had their own television, or at least the parents had their own in their bedroom. It was so easy for everyone to split up and watch the programs they wanted. The evening would go by and none of these families had spent time together and they never talked to each other. I decided that more important to me than watching my favorite program was wanting to raise my child to be loved and well adjusted. I wanted to spend the evening watching T.V. together with my children. This did several things. I got to see what programs Tami, Traci and Terri liked to watch and then I could determine whether they should be watching them or not. If we watched a program that had some questionable theme, we could discuss it. I could use that time to plant my seeds – again! If we watched the programs pertaining to teenagers, it would give the girls the opportunity to share with me that maybe those same things were going on at their school. We could discuss how they felt, and how they would handle it. I practically always let them watch the programs they wanted. Who cared? Television is an entertainment, not a time to tear the family apart. I wasn't going to be selfish and insist they didn't watch those silly programs and insist that they watch the news. The main purpose was for me to keep the communication open between Tami, Traci, Terri and me. And do you know what? If there was a special program on or I just thought we should listen to the news, the girls never got upset. They were always very agreeable. The girls appreciated so much that I was unselfish that they wanted to return the favor and be unselfish, to me. Over the years, I've noticed that if you take the full year of television programs into consideration, we all usually ended up getting a chance to watch our favorite programs. This is possible because of the rerun schedule. If we had been watching their programs throughout the year, that when April came, the girls would say, "Oh mom, this is a rerun of my program. Let's watch what you want to watch." Therefore, we watched the reruns of my favorite programs for the summer. No one lost out, we learned to be unselfish, to be considerate and we did things together. We shared lots of good laughs and times.

In another chapter, I've told you that I drove the girls in my car in practically all situations. It would have been much easier to have them catch a ride with a neighbor and, later, a classmate, but I wanted to be with my child whenever I could, even if only for a few minutes, so I could keep in touch with her. I wanted to use that time to talk to her, meet her friends and see where she'd be for the next hour. Remember, that when I had my girls I made conscious decisions about how I would raise them. I looked at kids I knew or had heard about who had been in trouble in their teen years or maybe didn't go to college and I made the decision that I would do everything to stay communicating with my child, knowing their friends, encouraging them and doing whatever I could to develop confidence. It was a conscious decision and I had a purpose. My purpose wasn't to be hovering over them and be a pest or nagging mother. In fact, I planned and did everything with much thought so the girls would have no idea of what I was doing. I was only concerned about the outcome of their life when they became adults. It definitely took a little extra gas, and I couldn't stay home and watch that T.V. program or read that best seller, but I was spending precious time with my daughters. This driving is so much easier, as a single parent. You don't have to feel you're neglecting your spouse at home. You have no priorities; just your child.

We were great in our family about writing notes. You might enjoy this habit as much as we did. Often, I'd write a little note and put it in the girls' lunch. Maybe they were concerned about a test, a speech, a friend or whatever it might be, and I just wrote a brief note of encouragement. I often just wrote that I'd be praying for her while she took that difficult test. Other times, I simply just told her, "I love you." When the girls went to camps or on trips, I often slipped a short letter in the top of their suitcases, so that when they got to their destination they'd know I was missing them but still so happy they were able to go on that excursion. In addition, I always wrote letters to the girls while they were out of town. I can remember when I was young and went away from home, that mail call was so exciting. It didn't matter what the letter said, it was just the excitement to get the mail. In Traci's junior year at Pepperdine, she went to Germany with about 50 classmates. They all lived together in the same mansion. She was quite apprehensive about being so far away from home, her mom and friends. Therefore, I decided to help her get adjusted by writing her letters every day. I decided to write her every day for 30 days, thinking that would give her time to make her own friends and get settled in Germany. After the letters began to arrive steadily, she called me to tell me how much she appreciated the mail. Later, she called to say how others envied her for getting mail and they thought her mom was so nice. Well, because she kept raving and appreciating the letters so much, how could I even think about stopping? It took me about 20 minutes a day to write that letter. Whenever I hesitated, I reminded myself that if Traci were living at home with me, I would have easily spent more than 20 minutes giving Traci my time. If those letters meant so much to Traci, I would continue writing them. I wrote Traci every day for those nine months. It cost me so little, but it meant so much. Note writing reversed itself, and the girls would always write me notes, particularly, if I had been out for the evening at a PTA meeting, a church meeting or a date, I would often even see a note greeting me on the door when I got home. Definitely, there was always an 'I Love You' note by the telephone. Those notes always meant so much to me.

When something needed fixing in the house, my first reaction was to panic. The second thought would be to try to think of a man who could help me. After a few seconds, I would realize I didn't know a man I wanted to impose upon, so I would ask my daughter, "Can you please read the instructions and try to fix the VCR? I'm sure you can do it. You are so smart." She would know I depended on her and, without fail, every time, that daughter was able to fix what needed fixing. As well as not having to impose on a man, I was instilling confidence in my daughter. I was also letting the girls know we could stick together and fix things. We were depending on each other and keeping those close family ties, instead of going outside the family.

Going to church was a necessary family tradition in our home. It is my belief that we all get our strength from somewhere, and I wasn't going to get mine from alcohol and drugs. I hadn't been successful at getting strength and security from men, so I decided that I would put my trust in God. I wanted to give the girls that same strength. We all committed to attending church regularly. Not only were we learning how to live better lives, but also we were doing and sharing something together. This was a wonderful way to keep the family close. I can't tell you how many times one of us would comment that the sermon really helped us through a problem or decision we were facing. We didn't live the life of "holier than thou", but we put our trust in somebody bigger than us. Before we set out to drive on a trip, I always prayed with the girls, in the car, asking the Lord to give us a safe trip. So often, I would drop the girls off and say, "Don't worry about that test or friend. You'll handle it all right. I'll be praying for you." Those prayers gave each of us confidence and strength to get through difficult times. If you agree that church is good for you and your family, you must commit to attending with your kids. If you want to keep close family ties, you have to agree to get up early and go with your children. We cannot expect out children to do something if we don't think it's good enough for us to do too. We must be the examples. As time goes by and those teenagers become so busy, there will be less and less time that you will see your child. Going to church will just be one way that you can be with that child and share some personal moments. It takes unselfish effort to have those family ties.

The evening meal is an excellent time to just sort of stop everything and sit at the table and eat together. I used to do this when I was married. It seemed less realistic now with just the girls and no dad in the house. We'd get home late from games or practice and we often picked up some food or stopped and ate someplace. However, I do think it's an excellent opportunity to share with your child. Even if you don't sit at the table to eat, and you simply sit in front of the television. The main thing is not where or what you are doing, but that you do it together. Don't use this mealtime to complain or discipline your child. You can control yourself to wait to bring up that sensitive matter until another time. Use this mealtime together to watch the news or perhaps one of those silly comedies that will make you laugh together. Laughing is great therapy and we should take every advantage to laugh with our children. Make mealtime a good time. Don't bring up a subject that might cause tension; there are other opportunities for that later.

I've shared with you just some examples of what I've done, and found to work, in keeping my family together. Each and every sharing time I've had with my daughters was much easier to have as a single parent. If I had a spouse, he might think some or much of my ideas were trivial. I didn't have to fight inside about whom to please, my husband or myself. It was easy. It was worth every effort I took. My kids are great. Be positive and hang in there as the single parent. It can be a good life for all of you.

YES, YOU CAN BE A GREAT SINGLE PARENT AND STILL DATE

Just because you want to make sure your children grow up happy and successful doesn't mean you can't have any personal time of your own. You need to date. Dating is one of the very positive, fun things about being single. One of the first things I noticed about being single is that I no longer had to worry about whether I was making my spouse happy or not. I think we all have worried about that when we were married. I also noticed that I would be asked out by men who thought I was wonderful. They admired me so much. Dates never criticized me. They would compliment me on how I was able to work, raise the girls by myself and be happy. These dates didn't realize that when they praised me, they were adding to my self-esteem. They were making me that happy person and, in turn, I would feel better about myself and be a better single parent. Dating is very important to we single parents. Just be wise.

During my many years of being a single parent I have dated dozens and dozens of times. Some of you might date less often because you become more seriously involved with one person. That didn't seem to happen in my situation. However, our hearts all react differently. The main thing I always kept foremost in my mind was that if I wanted to go out on a date, I would go; I would just adjust my dating schedule around the girls. My dates never seemed to mind. I think they actually respected me for having my priorities.

When the girls were little, I would be invited to go to dinner or a movie. I was excited. To me, it was always a boost to my ego to be asked out. After all, I had a husband desert me at one time. Then I had a husband severely mistreat me. Being asked out made me feel that I was still desirable company to have around. Some dates seemed to be really special and I looked

119

forward to them with great anticipation. I would dream and look forward to being with that man with lots of optimism. I would always think, 'Maybe this will be the right man.' However, there were many dates whom I knew weren't potential men for me to love, but they were nice friends. We could just have a good time together. Perhaps we would just be encouragers to each other. I would be just as excited to get to go out to dinner with these men. When I would be invited out, the date usually would ask, "What time would you like to go out?" This made it easy. I would respond with, "Well, by the time I get through work and get the girls after school, it's late. If you don't mind, I would like to have time to feed the girls, help them with their homework and get them settled for bed. Would 8 o'clock be O.K.?" I can't remember having a man get upset because I wanted to go out later. I did make sure I stayed awake all evening with my date though. Maybe the next night I would go to bed with the girls at 7:30 so I could catch up on my sleep. But I didn't want to short change my date. Even if my dates were on the weekends, I still wanted to leave after the girls were fed and ready for bed.

A difficult time for dating came when I would be invited for an all day excursion on Saturday or Sundays. Because I lived in Hawaii, I was often asked to go sailing for the day; or an event that maybe would only take half the day would be to play tennis. I would have loved to have gone; nevertheless, I would think of the girls. Remember how hectic the weekdays are. There isn't a lot of time to spend with the kids just relaxing -- there is getting home late, doing homework, cooking dinner and getting them settled early for bed. The weekend is when you can relax and just spend some precious time with the kids. I beg you to think of the children first. If your child is going to be away with the other parent, or if he is spending the night with a friend then that is when you can plan these all day or half day fun things. I do suggest that you don't make a big thing about it in front of the kids. For example, if you happened to be invited to go sailing one particular weekend and your child has no plans to be away from home, then just turn down the invitation. Your date should understand, even if he or she is disappointed. But, please don't even let your child know that you had to give something up for him. Don't try to get sympathy from the child. That would be selfish. It is your duty to be with your child while you are raising him. Remember, being a parent isn't just bringing children into the world and then ignoring them. What I would do is not mention anything if I decided not to go out and leave my girls. The funny thing is that whenever my girls have to leave me for the day or weekend they all would worry about me. They didn't want me to be alone. That's when I would say, "Oh, honey that is so thoughtful of you. Don't worry, though. I'm going to go on a picnic and hike with so and so. I'll be busy." They seemed relieved in those instances that I wouldn't be lonely. Don't you agree that if you just think it out and do it this way everyone is happy? You are completely free to date. Your child won't even have known you were gone. It seemed more important to spend Saturday taking the girls to the beach or zoo instead of me playing tennis. I had a goal in my life. I made that goal when the children were born. I wanted them to feel they were important people in this world. My goal wasn't to be a professional tennis player. It was too late for that. My goal wasn't to have the best-shaped body in the city. My goal wasn't to make all the men happy by accepting their date offers. My goal was to raise these children to be happy, well adjusted people as adults. If I went off and left them they would know they didn't matter much to me. I didn't think I would be helping their self- esteem if I left them with a babysitter to watch cartoons all day. I would always think that, no doubt, this man who was inviting me to the day's event would be out of my life in a couple months, and my children would never be out of my life. I needed to make an investment in either the man or the girls. I chose the girls. I always reminded myself that I wanted these children very much. They didn't ask to be born. I never dreamed of having to raise them alone. I had to put my personal wishes second. It was and is my belief that if we put others first then we will receive special blessings. If we do what we want selfishly, we will reap unhappiness in the long run. I never lacked in dates. I had great times. I just never neglected the girls.

There were even times during my 15-plus years of being a single parent that I was able to leave the children and get away for the weekend. I don't think this should be a regular happening. Your children need you to do things with them on weekends. However, there was one time I had an opportunity to go to Jamaica for a weekend. This invitation came at a time when I was struggling financially. It was soon after I left my second husband. I had been severely depressed. A businessman invited me to go with him and a few of his business partners while they mostly golfed. It was a real treat. I knew it would be uplifting to me. I would come back refreshed and be a better mother. I agreed to go and I explained all the details to the girls. They were happy for me. You see, if your children know that you have always put them first, they will want you to do something special for yourself. I was only gone four days and it did wonders for my attitude. There were a couple more short trips like this that I was able to take. Regardless, I would make arrangements for the girls to be left with excellent babysitters in more than adequate care. I would discuss with them who they would like to stay with while I was gone. I tried to make it a treat for my daughters, as it was a treat for me. Of course, I always called often to make certain I would be available for any problems or questions.

In Tami's high school years I heard of so many of her friends whose mothers or fathers just took off almost every weekend, often with different people. When these kids were in my home they talked about this. It is easy to see that these children were disappointed with their parents. They had no respect for their moms and dads. It is obvious to see why these parents had problems with their children obeying or communicating with them. The child didn't like what the parents did and couldn't respect them. It seemed clear to me that after the children were gone there would be plenty of weekends that you could go away on trips. At that time in your life, you will want to keep busy because there won't be any children in the home. You won't have to be an example to the son or daughter any more. They will be living their own lives. Your kids will want you to be happy and they won't want to be worrying about you. Those are also the weekends that you will have many free hours to sail and play tennis. You will have earned that freedom. I just don't feel I have earned that time to ignore my children until I have fulfilled my job of raising them completely.

The area of dating is one area where it is more difficult for the parent who has custody of the child. Sometimes it might seem unfair to you that your spouse can go and come whenever he or she wants. I had those feelings. However, the longer I lived the single life I realized that it might look glamorous to some (in fact it might actually be glamorous the first year or so), but that soon wears off. It's really lonely and frustrating out there. Don't you get discouraged and tired of going out on those dates with great anticipation, just to find out that this person isn't as great a date as you had imagined? It must be especially frustrating for the man if he has to pay for date after date, only to find out that none of the ladies are what he wants to take out for a second or third time. Most women just lose their time, not their money. It didn't take long for me to no longer envy my "ex" for all his freedom with dates. The girls brought me so much more moments of pleasure. I got to be a part of all their activities. My "ex" got none of that. I got to hear all their happenings. I got to be there for those first little phone calls from friends. I got to plan the birthday parties. I was there to see them go out on their dates. He had eight years of many dates and spending lots of money. I had eight years of watching the children grow and blossom and love me to death. I wouldn't trade the laughs, tears and discussions for anything. But that doesn't mean I don't want to be with a man -- I do. I hope that some day I will find that special companion. It looks like by the time I find that man, the girls will be all loved, educated and on their own. I will be ready to give all my time to this special man. My girls are not giving me any problems and they are secure emotionally. Two of my girls already have excellent careers. They have found good husbands who are as secure and educated as they are. It's my observation that most parents who put their own concerns first while they're raising the little children and teens have kids who grow up unable to cope with life. They're probably living on their own, but still asking for money, advice and attention. They never got it during those formative years, so they still need it when they should be able to take care of themselves. Doesn't it just make sense to take a few years to give all your efforts to raising that child as your investment? Then, when you're through with your job, you won't have any major worries. It's like any job. Do it right the first time and you won't have to do it again. Believe me, those child-rearing years will go by fast. You'll have plenty of time to sow those wild oats. If you don't do it right in the beginning, you may never have the freedom or extra money to sow those oats. You might end up giving it up to the kids even though they are 20 and 30.

Talking on the telephone is the same as dating. It doesn't make any sense to not go on a date so you can help your child with his homework and then you talk to your honey all the time. You can call your friend later in the evening. If you're staying home to help your child with his homework, then be there for him. Make those phone calls during the day or after he is in bed. That child needs your attention.

When Tami was about 15 she came home and said, "Mother, I am glad you aren't like other moms." I asked her what she meant. She said, "Like Kimberly's mom. We were in her bedroom and she has condoms lying all around." Now that is unnecessary! Even if you think your child knows you're having a relationship with someone, you don't have to flaunt it. A child has to allow you to do what you want. You are the parent. However, that doesn't mean they're proud of what you are doing. They might not voice an opinion, but they have their pride. I am not innocent by any means. However, I have class and do behave in a manner that wouldn't embarrass my daughters. It's worth it, to me. I wanted my daughters to be proud of me. Tami's not embarrassed to bring her friends to my bedroom. I keep remembering that there will be plenty of time later on to make other decisions with regards to my personal life.

As the children have become teenagers they have had special dates; maybe it was a first date; maybe a date with a new guy; maybe it's that yearly dance date. I want to be there to watch her dress. I want to tell her how pretty she looks. I want to help calm her when she's nervous. I want to meet the boy. Then I want to be there when she returns. I want to hear about the excitement as soon as she gets home. You know how it is when you have something exciting to tell someone. You want to tell them NOW. Something is lost in the excitement if you can't reach that person to tell the great news at this very moment. These would be the nights I would ask for a postponement of a date. It seems only common sense that a date would let me go out the next night or the next weekend so that I can share this special night with my daughter. They always have been very understanding. To be honest, if I was asked on a date and the man couldn't understand why I wanted to take a rain check on the date, then I would think he probably wouldn't understand a lot about me. I might as well not even waste my time with him. Oh, definitely! Many times I have been dying to go out with a particular man. I had to really fight being selfish and going. But later on when I saw the pleasure I brought my daughter when she knew I was staying home for her, it was worth it. It was also worth it when I realized two or three months later that I didn't care to date that man anymore. I can just guarantee you that in the future I would never have remembered how my date went, but I will never forget seeing my daughter go to that first prom, or with that special guy. I promise you that the next time I want to go out on a date, my daughter is excited for me to go. She never fails to appreciate that I was home for her when she needed me. Oh she doesn't go into this profound monologue, but I know.

I would like to make another suggestion with regards to your children and your dates; it's just something that I have observed and experienced. I really don't think it works too well to take your kids with you out on that second or third date. Oh, I know! You had one wonderful date. You think this guy or lady is really special. Perhaps you want to show off your kids and maybe there's that hope that all of you can soon be one "happy family" or maybe you want to show that special person that you like him or her so much that you want to include their children. All of these thoughts are excellent; They should work, however more times than not, it just doesn't seem to be a successful thing to do. My suggestion is to have several dates with your friend so that you know if the two of you hit it off real well. You two need time to get to know each other. It's just like when two people get married. It is usually recommended that a couple wait awhile to have children, so they can get adjusted to marriage. I think the same counsel would apply to dating. Don't get too excited to take the kids. What if the kids don't like mom or dad dating? That can cause tension --it could ruin a potentially good relationship between the two of you. If the two of you have become very good friends you will know how to work out these things later on. Otherwise, it could be just too much hassle, and one of you could get discouraged and not call for the other again. Also, this gives you time to make sure you really enjoy your new friend. After several dates, if you think there might be some future, then you can start sharing some things about this new person with your children. You will have time to prepare them. You will have time to assure them that they will always be first in your life. You can promise them that they won't be neglected. They will, in turn, be watching you go out on many dates. They will know you care about this person. I have really learned some

126

of this the hard way. It wasn't that I took my daughter along on the dates, but I would talk about each date with Tami. I wanted to include her in everything. I would tell her where I went on the date and I would tell her everything a man had told me about his life. I had thought it interesting and wanted to share with her. I could make it positive or negative depending what I thought. Nevertheless, when Tami got to be about 15 years old it became apparent to me that my daughter didn't think I had good judgment. It seemed that over the years I would think very positively about a man and within a few dates discovered that I had been wrong. I think Tami didn't respect my positive opinions of my dates any longer. I had made too many wrong opinions. She would just sort of turn me off. Then, when I would learn the man wasn't the right one for me, she would think 'There mother goes again. Not knowing how to choose the right men. I have to admit that Tami could usually see from the beginning whether the date was right for me or not, long before I could. The reason for that, I think, is that sometimes I just wanted to go out someplace special. There probably wouldn't be a future relationship, but that didn't mean I couldn't go out once and have a good time. Almost too late in her life, I've learned to just wait before I start telling Tami how great this guy is. Yes, you can, no doubt, see that I have not been the best judge of character. Actually, maybe I was, but I just didn't want to stay home and feel sorry for myself.

Whether to date or not is a decision you will have to make. I know some divorced people who just don't want to date, period. You can choose that. I don't think it will cause much harm when you're young. However, I know women who, as they get around 40, have turned down dates and soon wonder why there is no one to ask them out. These women seem to get very depressed as they get older. I chose to accept most dates. I could always be sure my date enjoyed my company. I'm a positive, intelligent, fun person. Then I would enjoy the conversation, dinner or movie; and, as I said earlier, to me it was an encouragement to

127

my self-esteem to be asked out on dates. I want to enjoy the company of men and dating as long as I am asked. The day will probably come when those invitations stop coming my way.

Don't let your children put the guilt on you for dating. You need to make wise decisions and not neglect the kids; but a little child has no authority to make you feel guilty for dating. I have watched little ones throw temper tantrums when mom prepares to leave with a date; or maybe it has been a sullen, pouty face when the date shows up at the door. Even more importantly, you must not let the child control whom you could potentially marry. You need to "nip it in the bud" when you see these signs -- and you will. All kids play parents and people against each other. Be firm. Punish the child for acting in an inappropriate manner. Please take some suggestions from other chapters as to how to discipline the child who causes you trouble. You be the boss. You must be consistent.

After you have dated quite awhile and you begin to think you are falling in love, you very possibly might want to remarry. This is great! If you found a person who loves you and your children the way you do, then nothing could be better for you. Raising children with two parents can be the most enjoyable. You can have the best of both worlds. This is the way life should be. It just doesn't happen too often. And I want you to know, you don't have to marry just anybody to give your child a mother or father. You can be the single parent and do it almost perfectly. It's much better to raise your children alone and give them happiness than to marry the wrong person. I have heard it said one time and I loved it, "It's better to want what you don't have then to have what you don't want." Marriage is not worth it if there is always tension or you are caught in the middle of the children and your spouse. You can, raise your child as a single parent, and still have fun with you own dates.

THE MOST IMPORTANT THING YOU CAN GIVE YOUR CHILD IS NOT LOVE

Does this surprise you? Haven't we all heard that the most important thing we can do for our child is to love them? Whenever I'm in a group of parents I hear them say they love their kids. In fact, I dare say, I've never heard any parents say they don't love their children. If everyone is loving their kids then could you tell me why so many kids are growing up feeling so unloved and insecure?

Perhaps some of you, like me, have been in a relationship where the spouse or partner insisted he or she loved you. Our response has been, "But you don't show it!" If I was loved, why didn't I feel it? Why wasn't I happier? As an example, when I've interviewed men about their relationships with their wives, they've said to me, "Ginger, I can't understand why my wife is so unhappy. I have a good job, and I bring home the money and give it all to her. I'm faithful to her. She doesn't have to worry about a thing." We women want more, don't we? We appreciate the money, but we know we could get a job to take care of ourselves financially. We just want more than love from our partner. It's at that moment in our relationship when we sit down with our special someone and try to explain what we want from him. It has been told me by these very men, "We men want to feel loved too. We have needs." Women will argue that they do show the man they love him. They say, "I do love him. I cook for him. I clean the house and take care of the kids. I am faithful. What else can I do?" Men will argue, "But I need more."

There is no doubt that my second husband loved our daughters. He adopted the older two because he wanted them to feel a part of the unity of the family. He wanted his own little child so much. But the girls, to this day, are not happy with how their dad treated them. They did not respect him as a father. They

129

do not feel they received what a child needs from a father. His way of showing love was not what they needed to feel loved. It's a shame that he hadn't learned how to properly show his love. He never learned what is the most important thing in being a father.

The most important thing you can give your child is TIME. This is probably one of the most difficult contributions we can make. It takes a sacrifice. One cannot be of a selfish nature and still give his child TIME. Are you one who says, 'I provide for my child financially, so that verifies I love him. I'm not neglecting my responsibility'. It takes little sacrifice to provide the necessary money for the children. Think about it -- even if you didn't have any children, you would still have to pay rent, utilities, car payments and food for you and your spouse. You might choose to spend a lot of extra money on your child, giving him better things and opportunities, but you and your child could survive without the material items. Your son or daughter could still grow up to be happy, secure, loved and a well-adjusted adult. Many successful people are products of poverty. On the other hand, many children who have not had enough TIME given to them have turned out to feel very unloved and are pretty unhappy people in our world. These are the adults sitting on the psychologist's couches, with a breaking heart, feeling that they weren't loved or special. Perhaps you are even one of those individuals. These are the people who don't feel good about themselves and they lack strength. When they come to a difficult time in their life they don't have what it takes to get through it.

If you really want to help your child to grow up to face the world and the problems in it, you are going to have to put your child before that tennis game. You might not be able to attend that aerobics class three times a week. Maybe you will have to drop your membership from one of those community organizations. And for you church people, you will undoubtedly have to say "no" to being on that committee. In our society, we are obsessed with having a good heart rate. Many people would never think of missing that 6:00 P.M. hour of exercise to keep their metabolism at the correct rate. I have yet to meet a parent who is so determined to give that same regular time to a child. We are consumed with joining an organization so we can be with our friends, be in the right group, or perhaps to network.

Why is it we have to give excuses for wanting to spend an extra hour or evening with our children, but we never apologize for "having to" take that walk or run? Can you even begin to imagine what our next generation would be like if we were as concerned with our children's well being as our heart rate. I'm told that by increasing your exercise and eating a low-fat diet, you might increase your life span three years. That's fine, if you have the desire. Wouldn't it be a much better investment to give those extra hours to your child as he is going to contribute, either good or bad, to our society, for 50 to 75 years? Personally, I wouldn't want to live an extra three years watching my child and others suffer, when I know they could be much better people if I had given them more of my time. Time is much easier to give your child if you are a single parent than if you are a married parent. The only thing it really takes is unselfishness. You will only have to have your priorities in the right place.

Time can be given in many different ways. If your child is small and taking lessons, you should stay and watch him if possible. Those little tykes are so excited when they do that first tumble, or play that first tune all the way through without any mistakes. It's just not as effective when he or the teacher has to tell you, after that tumble has transpired, how well he did. So much of the excitement is lost. You can be in the room and still write or visit with people, but your child knows you are there. You are also listening as to how the teacher treats your child. If you weren't observing, you might not understand when your child says "Mommy, the teacher doesn't understand why I can't do it." Your child needs you to know what is going on, so you

131

can encourage him. Then, too, if you have seen that great performance of your child, you have more of a tendency to boast to the family and your friends about him. This will be a contribution to his self-esteem. When that little one wants you to read to him, you must take the time to stop what you are doing to read. Just how long does it take to read one of those children's books -- maybe five minutes? How difficult is it for you to wait on the laundry or making that phone call for those five minutes? It really won't hurt you at all, and at the same time you're giving time to your child and letting him know he's the most important thing to you. As the child grows older, he will want to talk to you. You need to wipe your hands on that dishtowel and listen to him. Sit down and look at his school paper. Read it over. Notice things about it so that you can add to the conversation. Don't be like some parents, whose kids have told me, "My mom acts like she cares, but I know she didn't really read or look at it. My mom is too busy." It is also very important that you attend every PTA meeting. Sure, this can be difficult, particularly, if you've already been through this with one or two previous children. It's not fair for you not to give as much time to the second, third and fourth children as you did the first. I know you're tired after working all day. Regardless, we must remember what our main purpose is in this world. Isn't it to raise our children to feel loved and well adjusted? Don't we want them to be self-sufficient adults? So many times, I've been so tired that I didn't think I could make that PTA meeting. I felt literally exhausted. Still, I never questioned whether I would attend the meeting or not. I committed to these children when they were born. I never missed a PTA meeting for all three. I would just drag myself to the microwave for another cup of coffee and force myself to the car. When I got to the meeting, it was better. I actually found them relaxing. After all, I wasn't looking at the housework that had to be done. I would see the work my child had done and I would remember something, so I could discuss her work and teachers with her when I got home. I would bet that, without exception, every time I arrived home from the PTA meeting and I found something good to say about my daughter, her eyes would just sparkle. That was the best hour and a half of that month. I was contributing to my child's good self-esteem. And do you know what often happens to those dirty dishes or to all those clothes that were left in the dryer? Many times the girls had done the work for me. As they got older, I could ask them, "Please fold the clothes as mother is going to the PTA meeting." Your children will never complain about helping out if they know you are going to an event for them. When your children want to see a movie or go roller- skating, you should go with them. Of course, if you don't have much money, you can't do everything a little child requests. If you don't have the money, realize that they often just want your attention. Then it is the perfect time to suggest playing a game together or begin working on a puzzle. However, once a month or so you can spend that extra money to do something special. Do it with him. Don't leave him at the theater and pick him up. He needs to know that you care enough to spend the time with him. That counts, to him, as much or more than the movie. If you don't roller skate, you can just sit and watch. The main thing is to give that hour or two to your child. And, please, never complain about what you could be doing. Don't ever say to the child how much you are giving up to take him out. If you complain, you have just destroyed all that self-esteem you have been trying to instill -- you might as well not be going with your child at all. Think about how you are with your best friends; you want them to go or do things with you because they think it will be fun. Wouldn't you be miserable if your friend would say, "I hope you appreciate that I'm going with you. I could be doing something else. I'm always doing things for you." Naturally, we wouldn't like those types of friends. We seem to not realize that we are giving our child the same feelings when we complain. The time you spent with your child will be worthless if you so much as whisper a complaint. Tami often tells me, "Mom, I'm sorry you had to take me or go pick that item up for me." Now if my response was "Yeh, well, I don't have the time to do it and next time I won't," do you think she would be noticing the time I spend and would she be grateful? No way! I might as well have never done it. Once, Tami called me and said, "Mother, I'm so sorry. I had my P.E. clothes ready to go, but I was so rushed getting other things that I completely forgot them. If I don't have them, I'll be punished in P.E. Would you please bring them to me?" I rushed around and ran her clothes up to the school office on my lunch hour. She was waiting for me and so appreciative. I hugged her and didn't give one word of complaint. What good would it do? She felt terrible! However, it doesn't go unnoticed. Possibly, that evening while we are calm and watching T.V., I might ask her, "Hey, what made you forget your clothes this morning? Have you thought about what you will do, so that doesn't happen again?" Enough has been said. Other times, I have just waited until the evening before the next time she has to take her P.E. clothes to school, and I give her the following suggestion, "Tami, Your P.E. clothes are by your school bag. Now, please don't forget them in the morning like you did last week." Enough said! Haven't you and I forgotten something at home, and we had to fumble with excuses or go back and get it before that special meeting? Weren't we embarrassed and irritated with ourselves? Well, our children feel the same way, and they haven't had as many years as we've had to try to get into a memory habit. It's so worth our while to spend the time to take the item to our children whenever at all possible, without complaining. It's so much easier to teach them a learning lesson in a calm, positive attitude than to yell or grumble like some parents would do.

It seems like the hardest years for most parents to enjoy their children are the ages of about 7 to 12. When our babies were born, they were so cute! It was so much fun to brag about how quickly they walked, talked, cut teeth and were potty trained. Even through the preschool years and first grade, the kids are so much enjoyment. They are becoming more aware of the world and they say such 'adorable things.' Then, all of a sudden, they aren't quite so cute; they're losing teeth or will soon need braces.

They get dirty and their hair never stays neat and clean. They begin to try to talk back. Nothing seems to make them happy. It becomes difficult to really know what to do with them. We just sort of make a subconscious decision to hang in there to see what happens. To me, this is a very critical time. This is where you will lose touch with your child or you will keep a connection with him or her. You must remember that even though your child doesn't express all the positive comments to us that we'd like to hear, we are investing in the future. Even though we are not getting daily rewards, and we think our being there is a waste of time, we are making an impact on our child. We must hang in there and give our time to that child. If you slip up, then all of a sudden, in about the seventh or eighth grade, you will receive a phone call from the school counselor that your child isn't doing too well in school. Perhaps you will be told that your child has been involved in cutting classes, getting into fights or maybe even involved in drinking, smoking or drugs. You will be shocked! You won't have any idea how all this happened. You will have lost control. It will be too late then for you to begin to take over. At that stage of life, you'll just have to prepare yourself for doing your best to get him through school, period! However, if you stay interested in your child through those in-between years -- showing your child you care by giving your time -- I promise you that you will not have any negative calls from the school. Keep encouraging that young child to participate in school activities. Tell them, you will go with him, and even wait in the car if he doesn't want mother or dad hanging around. Let him know that you are there, so he can run to you in the car and tell you his problems. Trying out for a competitive sport can be very scary. I want to tell you what I did for Kelly, a darling girl, whom I considered almost my daughter. She was a freshman and had recently moved to Carmel to live with her dad. Her mother lived in Iowa. Kelly was so very anxious to try out for the softball team. She was new to the area and she knew that competition was tough. She wanted to play for herself; but also to please her brother, who was playing baseball

135

at college; and to please her dad, who was a coach. She practiced and practiced. The day of tryouts came. She was so nervous she was actually sick. I encouraged her. I noticed she was even shaking. I offered, "Kelly, I'll walk down to the field with you and introduce you to the coach." I watched for a response. She was very pleased. I hadn't met the coach before, but I said, "Hi, I'm Ginger and this is Kelly. Kelly is a good athlete and I know she will be an asset to your team." He was warm and friendly, and they walked over to the field. Before they left, I said, "Kelly, I'll be waiting for you up in the parking lot. I'll pray for you. I know you'll do it." She later told me how much better she felt because I walked her to the field, and then because she knew I cared and was waiting for her. What did that take from me? About 20 minutes of my time. She made the team. She was still shaking. She has told me she will never forget what I did for her. Get to know your child's teachers, coaches and friends. If your child has a special science project and needs extra materials, tell him you will take him to get them. Ask him to just make a list of what he needs. Let him know you will let the work on the car go on Saturday, or the housework will wait on Saturday, while you take your child to the stream to collect bugs. Give him your time. Never say, "You can do it yourself." Just be near that little person.

Traci wanted me to tell you readers about something I did for her that she considers special and it seems she will always remember. We happened to be living in Texas for a couple of years, when she was a 10th grader. I had to quickly go to Hawaii for a short business trip. There was no way out of it. Traci began to kind of panic, because she needed to spend that week getting different types of leaves for a science project. While I was gone she had no one to help her, and Texas doesn't really have that many trees or bushes. I assured her I would get her leaves in Hawaii. She probably had her doubts. However, as soon as my business meeting was over, the day I arrived in Hawaii, I immediately drove around and up the mountain. I gathered about

30 different kinds of leaves. I then rushed to the Federal Express office and sent her those leaves. She got them the next day, just in time to put together her project. She was thrilled. She still remembers what she thinks was a big effort. Actually, it probably took only about 20 minutes to get all those leaves. The Federal Express, no doubt, cost about $17.00. Let me tell you the time was worth it to help build my daughter's self-esteem. She knew I loved her. No matter what your child wants you to do that takes your time, I firmly believe you should do it. Some things will seem so silly to you. You will often think it is so trivial -- and it really is. Nevertheless, it's not the activity that you're participating in that will effect your child, but the fact that you're giving your child your time. I think you can even have a child in your home that you don't really love, but you can give him or her your time. There are many circumstances possible for you having the child, but you aren't too happy about it. Perhaps you've agreed to raise someone's child, as the parent is no longer around. Your commitment deserves a lot of credit. You want that child to turn out to be well adjusted to living in the world, but you just don't love him. You don't want your feelings to show, and you want to do the best job you can of raising that child. That's O.K. Don't feel guilty or bad about that. Just please spend time with that child. Granted, it is more difficult to spend time with children if you don't love them; however, it can be done, and without too much of a problem. While you're watching that child perform, you can be reading or visiting. When you have to run that child to a particular place, just think positively, that this was part of your commitment to raise that child. You're helping him to stand on his own feet, and he will, sooner than you realize, be living outside your house. It's all in the attitude, so please make sure yours is right. You will be a happier person for having a happy, positive attitude.

Something else I did as a single parent, was to comply with Tami's request, when she was in about the 4 th grade, for me to read all her Babysitters Club books. Now I am certain that you are roaring with laughter, just to think an adult read those books. She read them all and, as each new one came out, she asked to go to the bookstore to buy the most recent paperback. When she asked me to read them, I was rather taken back. I couldn't help but think of all the adult, intelligent books I should be reading. (I am certain that, had I been married, my husband would have either laughed at me or wanted me to read his suggestions). It was at that point, that Tami came up with a brilliant suggestion; She said, "Mother, you always read when you're on the toilet, so why don't you just read the Babysitter's Club Book then?" I couldn't deny the fact that while I sat on the toilet I did look at unimportant magazines. So, for Tami, why couldn't I read her books? I agreed, and she was thrilled, because she would be able talk to me about the girls in the book; and all their trials and friendships. Actually, this time was very well spent. The girls in the books were going through what every other little girl who is about 10, 11 and 12 goes through. It helped me to realize the situations Tami was facing with her friends. I would discuss them with her and used many opportunities to plant my seeds. This all might have seemed like a waste of time, but Tami thought it was the neatest thing that her mother cared enough to spend the time to read her books. She would tell all her friends. I spent a very few minutes every day and it took probably about five months to get them read. That time doesn't seem like much of a sacrifice to help my child feel loved.

Sharing how I spent time with my girls is, I hope, a way to give you ideas of how you can spend time with your children. Each child will have different needs. The most important thing is that you give your time willingly. You have much more time as a single parent. How many times I have done something for my daughters and then said, "Oh, it's late. I'm tired. I'm just going to leave the dishes and go to bed." I could do whatever I wanted. I was afraid to leave the dishes when I was married, as I didn't want my husband to think I was a slob. My child didn't think I was a slob, she just thought she was more important than the dishes. In fact, my girls knew they were the most important thing in the world to me. They always knew I would give them my time for any reason. Time is definitely the most important thing you can give your child. If you give your time sacrificially, your child will know you love him or her. If you have previously said you love your child, and not given the time you should, your child will not believe you really love him. Remember that old saying, "Actions speak louder than words."

HOW CAN I WORK AND STILL BE A GOOD PARENT?

It is so difficult to be Super Dad or Super Mom, isn't it? It's exhausting to be everything to everyone. It's so frustrating to try to make everyone happy -- YOU CAN'T! You don't have to be the one to make the world go around. However, you do have to provide financially and you do have to raise those children to the best of your ability. That is what you have to do! You can do this if you put priorities on your interests. The positive side of being a single parent is that you will have more time to give your children, because you don't have to worry about making a spouse happy. Therefore, look for the positive in your situation, instead of whining that you don't have someone to love you. Use this time alone to concentrate on those children to raise them with high self-esteem, goals, discipline, lots of time and love. There is plenty of time for you to be loved. When the time is right, that other person will come into your life. Remember that another man or woman might not want to develop a special relationship with you if your kids are into trouble or are not disciplined. So use these times to prepare for the future and while we're working we're teaching the children that we have certain responsibilities we must keep.

Yes, you can work and still be a good parent. Your child won't complain about you working, as long as you're spending valuable time with him. Children know that we have to work if we want to put food on the table. That child would not be proud of us if we weren't working. Children of parents who are unemployed are very embarrassed. As much as being embarrassed, these kids are hurting for us, because we can't provide for them like we want. The element of working is not a problem. By working, we are being good examples to our child. We are making another effort to increase our child's self-esteem. However, even though we will be working, we must recognize that we might not be able to climb the ladder as much or as fast or work the long hours we might be tempted to do. I had the advantage of being self-employed. The benefit of being self-employed is that I could adjust my own hours. However, there is even a bigger disadvantage of being self-employed and that is the pressure of knowing you should be working more hours. As self-employed people we know that if we leave work in the afternoon to go to watch our child play a basketball game, we might not make the sale we need to pay the rent. There is constant stress on a self-employed person. They carry a lot of guilt that they must fight. People who are employed at a regular nine to five job, know that they are to go home at five and there is nothing more that they can do with regards to their work -- they can go home and relax for the evening. There are exceptions, as there are the many professional people whose obligations can go with them throughout the entire 24 hours. We all have different situations with pros and cons. We have to adjust and just remember our priorities; our children and our jobs.

Perhaps you have that job with a nine to five schedule, which means you couldn't attend that sporting event if the game starts at 4:00. There are ways to get around this. More and more employers are realizing that it is very important for parents to spend time with their children. It also seems that employers are more understanding with a single parent family. Perhaps on the particular day of a game, you could ask your boss if you could come in an hour earlier, so that you could go home earlier. Maybe you can arrange with another employee to work for him an extra hour or two, if he will work for you on a particular day. People in your office or your employer might not appreciate it if you got special advantages too often, but maybe if you explained that this would only be going on for three months, say during baseball or volleyball season. And maybe you couldn't leave early more than one day a week but ask! It never hurts to ask. People all seem to want to help out if it is for kids. It's a lot different to ask for an adjustment to your work schedule if it's for your kids than if you want to go get your hair done. You need to save the requests for special favors, so that you can use them for your children. Even if you must have your hair appointment later in the evening, while your child is doing his homework or watching T.V., you can say, "Son, I'm sorry that I have to leave you for about an hour now; it's because I canceled my appointment earlier as I wanted to watch your game, but I just must get my hair done now." This won't hurt your son's feelings. He'll be glad to be left alone or with a babysitter for that hour, because he's so thrilled that you adjusted your schedule to watch his game. The main thing is that you THINK about what you can do. Never be afraid to ask. In every aspects of life we are told to ask. That is how we get smarter and how we learn and get further ahead in life. Now just suppose that perhaps you are possibly a policeman, and there is no way you can get off work to see the game. First, there is the possibility that you could exchange days off with another officer, just for this season, while your child is participating. However, if absolutely nothing can be done for you to participate, then you will need to go overboard, to sit down with your son at the soonest opportunity and ask for all the details of his game. Explain how broken-hearted you are that you couldn't watch him. But if you will just listen and give your undivided attention for 10 or 20 minutes, you will be contributing to his enthusiasm. If it's a basketball game that you are unable to attend, then make sure you sit with your son and watch the games on T.V. Talk about it with him and ask what he does. Sometimes, take him to another basketball game, just to show your are interested in the sport he plays. Always let your son know how frustrated you are that you can't attend his game. Tell him how proud you are of him. Remind him, that the only reason you aren't there is because your boss won't let you leave. Be very honest. Your son will be disappointed, but he will learn to accept situations if you have legitimate reasons. Kids just can't accept parents who don't come to their activities because they're lazy or selfish by putting other things before them. Perhaps you can get a grandparent or another parent or even the youth worker at church to rather adopt your child at these special events. You can check with this person over the phone, to show your child you're sincerely interested.

There are companies these days that have day care facilities available for families. This is great for especially the single parents. If you're just beginning to look for work as a single parent with a little one, then try to find a job where there is day care. Don't hesitate to ask. Perhaps they don't have one yet, but they might understand your situation and let you leave for lunch hour to visit your baby. Most employers are parents too. These same employers are very sympathetic toward single parents. They often have trouble getting good employees because of day care or baby-sitting problems. They also know how much it costs for these facilities.

The professionals who have to be on call all the time just has to go with the flow. They usually have a beeper or cellular telephone so that they can be reached at any time. If you are one of these, just begin by going to your child's event. If you get called away, even within the first ten minutes, your child will realize that you made a good attempt. The effort is what impresses your children. Sure, they will be disappointed if you can't stay the full time, but they can't blame you, because you tried. Naturally, you want to try to not have that beeper or phone go off every time. You will need to use discernment as to the importance of the call. Very possibly, you can tell the caller that you are tied up for the next 30 or 40 minutes, so you won't be able to meet until then. Just always think, 'Is my rushing there a necessity to the rest of my future or is it important that, this time, I stay right here with my child?' Remember the priority is your child. After he has gone to college, you can rush to those calls all the time.

The self-employed have to use the most discipline. They don't have a boss to control their hours or schedule. Nevertheless, you are the most disciplined, because you couldn't be self-employed if you weren't. You just have to learn to control the guilt, -- and the appointments. When I first went into real estate, at 29 years of age, my broker gave me some advice that has stuck with me for years. First of all, she said, "You must take a day off." I had previously been on welfare and I wanted to make certain I stayed off that system. She insisted, that we don't work for one day during the week. However, she said, you can take your business cards and, while you're lying on the beach, pass them out. I took her instructions to heart. By always being free to talk and pass out those business cards, it took the guilt away. I always actually thought I was working. Take that day and make certain to spend it with your kids. If you do feel you should be working, you can still talk and pass out those cards to the restaurant waitress, the sales clerk, the person next to you at the beach and just about anywhere. I was always surprised that I often picked up a client when I was least expecting it. At the end of that day off I would almost think that God gave me that "good lead" that day, to reward me for spending time with my girls. The other lesson I learned from my broker was that if you are going to do something with your children at 3:00, you just tell a perspective client, "I am sorry, but I have another appointment and won't be able to meet with you at that time. How about 2:00 or 5:00?" When I was first told to use this system, my little innocent heart made me think that was lying. However, Marie, my broker, went on to explain that meeting your child or picking him up after school is a definite appointment. You never have to tell your client with whom you have the appointment. I used this method so that I was always able to pick up my girls from school. There were times I would just have to drop them for the ice skating lesson or at home to do their homework, but I at least got to hear about what happened at school while we drove in the car and then was able to get them settled for the next hour or two. As the girls got older, they would have activities in the

145

afternoons that I wanted to be a part of, so I would do everything within my power to not have any appointments after 3:00 P.M. Actually, it was very easy. I would just tell the client that the afternoon was very busy -- how about if we meet first thing in the morning? My broker reminded us that we are never able to see the doctor or lawyer when we want. They are very busy people and they don't drop everything to see us immediately. We are professional people in our own field and we can control our schedule. There used to be the fear that I would lose a sale if I didn't do it "right now." But I don't believe I ever lost a sale for that reason. I was always sincere with my reason and I worked extra hard to show my credibility when I did meet with my client. I think it is true, that if you do cut your day short because of your child, you will work extra hard to make up for it. Besides, if you sat in the office, waiting for the phone to ring, instead of being with your child, what probably would have happened? I can tell you: You would have wasted the day chit-chatting with office people. You would have left, at the end of the day, and been frustrated that you didn't accomplish anything at work, and that you didn't get to see your child perform.

You might not be as successful in the work field or in the community because you've adjusted your schedule to be with your children. I have no doubt that I could have made more money and had a big name around town if I had worked more hours. I just had my priorities in another place. I was counting on more than financial rewards. What good is all that extra money if you end up using it to pay for your child's drug and alcohol rehabilitation? What good is that money if your child doesn't have good self-esteem and doesn't go on to be able to take care of himself financially and you end up supporting him and perhaps a spouse and a child or two? I want to share with you an anonymous poem that I have carried in my wallet all these years. It is my motto. Maybe it can be your motto as well. It has always helped for me to read it when I begin to worry about my financial situation.

146

When you're speaking of success.
You can measure it in a fancy home,
Expensive car or dress.
But the measure of your real success
Is the one you cannot spend.
It's the way your kids describe you
When they're talking to a friend.

What will your kids, as teenagers and later as young adults,
say about you?

YOUR REWARD -- INCLUDES THE
FINANCIAL GAIN!

If you give your child the time, build up his self-esteem, be positive in your attitude, discipline with consistency, treat him with respect, don't forget how it was when you were a child and be completely unselfish, you will be making money after your child graduates from college. If you are a young parent, no doubt you, cannot comprehend how this can be, but I will explain how it worked for me. However, the financial part is only one way in which parents receive a reward for raising their children in the proper way.

The fact of making money after my children were gone from the house recently became very real to me, when I begin to look around at my friend's kids, who are also grown. Then I look at my Terri, Traci and Tami. Invariably, most of my friend's and acquaintance's kids are well into their 20's and are still asking mom and dad to help them financially. The kids who don't have the self-esteem and didn't have the encouragement to finish college are doing the minimal jobs. When they need a new car, because the old one broke down, these kids aren't making enough money to qualify for the loan. Their mom and dad are asked to co-sign for the financial note and often even asked to help with a down payment. I have seen parents feel sorry that their children can't buy any new clothes because their salary is so low and the parents are still buying them clothes. Parents have helped with gas and airline tickets so their child can go on a trip with friend or relatives. Many of these same children have not waited to get married until they could provide for a family, and now they have little babies. These parents are buying the much needed items for their new grandchildren. My friend's financial responsibilities did not stop, or even come to a halt, when their child turned 18, 20 or even 25. The money the parents had planned to enjoy for themselves, after their children were out of

149

their home and on their own, is still being spent on the children and the grandchildren.

Terri went to the University of Kansas and she drove around the large campus on a moped. I often felt sorry for her. When she graduated with a B.S. in Pharmacy, she came home, got a job right away and she quickly went down and bought a new red Acura. This was the first year Acuras were sold. I was so delighted for Terri. The following year, Terri and Guill prepared for their wedding. I had very much wanted to pay for the wedding. I'm from the "old school" and I had always dreamed of paying, as is the custom for the bride's family. Unfortunately, around the time of their wedding plans, I could hardly survive myself, financially. I had to tell the kids I was sorry I couldn't help them pay for the wedding. Because both she and Guill expected to pay, and had excellent jobs, they handled all the finances. They had one of the most beautiful and expensive weddings that any two people could plan.

Traci had no car, except for one year, at Pepperdine. That car was her grandmother's old, old Buick. She certainly didn't fit in to the look of Pepperdine, with all of the BMWs and Ferraris. Many times, her car didn't even start, but she made it through college with flying colors. Her last year, she had made enough money working that she could handle small payments. She was able to buy a Honda Civic. She and Jeff began to plan their wedding, and I still wasn't in a financial position to help. I was extremely disappointed that I couldn't contribute to another daughter's wedding. They didn't expect me to pay for anything and, fortunately, Jeff had been out of college for one year and had an excellent job. He was able to pay for what was another of the most beautiful and expensive weddings that one has ever attended. They paid for everything without any substantial financial help from either set of parents.

If these kids hadn't graduated from colleges, they chose carefully, with professional degrees, they would not have been able to pay for their own weddings. Also, if they hadn't met and planned to marry educated men, who had good jobs before they got married, they would not have been able to have such big and beautiful weddings. This saved me a lot of disappointment and stress. Many parents have to help their children pay for the wedding, and many don't even want to help like I really did. Still there are other couples who would love to have a beautiful wedding, but they can't afford it and neither can their parents. They have to forego their dreams. What a shame!

Terri and Guill bought a house after three years of working toward their goals, which included paying off school loans. Guill has his own computer business and except for one day a week, Terri is a stay-at-home mom with their two children. Traci and Jeff have almost paid off their school loans and after living in Europe for four years, they returned to America, where Jeff has an excellent job in the Silicon Valley and they live in the San Francisco Bay area where Traci is a stay-at-home mom with their two children. Neither couple has ever asked me for one penny. On the contrary, they have helped me when my situation has been a little rough. Not only that, but my sons-in-law have consistently told me that they will always make sure I am taken care of if I can't provide for myself. They have also, all these years, told me they would take care of Tami financially and emotionally if something happened to me before she graduated and got out on her own. Many sons or daughters might offer, but very few could actually provide, should that be necessary.

Financial gains are not the most important reward you will receive from giving unselfishly to your child. And you don't have to wait until your child graduates from college to receive your rewards. The rewards will be daily.

One of those rewards will happen when it's time for you to attend the PTA; you'll love to go. You'll be so proud when the teachers tell you how well your child is doing. I feel so sad for other parents who have to sort of corner the teacher and ask about their child. On the other hand, you'll be bursting with pride when the teacher says to you, "I wish all my students were as good as yours. If they were, I would have no problems whatsoever."

Probably the best reward that keeps me going daily, when I begin to think things are rough, is that, everywhere I go, people come up to me and say, "I saw Terri, (or Traci or Tami). She is such a sweet girl. She is just something very special and unusual. You have certainly done a wonderful job being a single parent. I wish I knew your secret." These statements go on and on. I can bet my life on it, every time -- if I run into someone who has met my girls, they will say almost the exact same thing. Well, you now know my secret, and you can do the same -- if you want. I'll tell you, I would take compliments like this every day, or even once a week, rather than for someone to tell me, "You can play a great tennis game." Or to say, "You're so slim and in such good shape. It must come from working out at the gym every day." It's where my priorities were set, and you must begin to think now just what is your desire in life. Believe me, I know many people who can play a great game of golf or tennis and their bodies look in fantastic shape, but they don't have self sufficient grown children and they still haven't found that special someone to love and perhaps marry.

Another very important reward for you is that you won't ever have to worry about your child being sexually harassed, which is something we hear a lot about these days. Your child will feel confident about herself (this is particular for girls, but could definitely also apply to boys). She will be able to stand on her own and won't let people harass her. Your child won't be sexually abused by a friend, stranger or a member of the family.

You will have talked so openly and freely with your children, that they will know that those sex acts aren't right and they won't allow it. Your kids will know that you'll believe them, because they know you love them as you given them so much of your time and attention. When that child gets out in the work force, there will never be an opportunity for an employer to threaten your child with sexual harassment. Your child will either know how to handle the situation or, with confidence, he can quit knowing he feels good enough about himself that he will be able to get another job.

Terri, Traci and Tami never talk back to me or embarrass me in front of my friends. This is a constant reward, and one of my favorites. My heart aches for parents whose kids sass them in front of everyone. What a humiliating thing to have your 6-year-old, 12-year-old or even your 20-year-old talk back to you. It has never happened to me. When they were very little, I wouldn't allow it. Now, they'd never think of doing it. They respect me and love me very much.

Your child will have such high self-esteem because he got a good college education. He will be confident that he can get a good job. Even when the economy becomes bad your child will know that it is not because of anything he has or hasn't done, that he can't get employment. He won't take it personally, and he'll know it's just due to the low economic conditions in that particular city or even in the entire country. If your child didn't feel confident about himself, he would just take any job and be unhappy and unsatisfied all his life. You would always be trying to help him and encourage him. He would drain you emotionally. I have never had to give Terri and Traci any extra word of encouragement. I just continually praise them and tell them how proud I am. They are very self-confident and satisfied when they are working. They know they're doing the best that can be done.

All those years, we worry that our children will marry too young or the wrong person. Perhaps we remember when and why we got married, and probably later divorced. We don't want our children to make the same mistakes. We spend so many hours worrying. There is definitely no guarantee for a happy and long marriage, but we want so badly for our kids to do better than us, don't we? Well, they will, undoubtedly, have an improved chance at a successful marriage if they aren't unhappy at home and anxiously waiting to get away from mom and/or dad. They'll wait for that superior partner if they feel healthy about themselves and they will know they deserve the finest. They won't ever think, 'This is the best I can do.' They'll know they don't have to get married soon, for fear of losing out on love. They'll be more intelligent by getting that college degree and letting a few years of maturing get under their belts. They will want to wait to get married until they know they can contribute to the support of a family. None of this eludes the fact that the person we often think is our ideal marriage partner at 18 years is often not the same one we would choose at 25 years. If your child postpones wedding plans and takes marriage seriously, you won't have your kids whining to you about their unhappiness. So many of my acquaintance's kids are so frustrated. Some of their spouses don't help each other out in the family situations, while others are abusive. There are just all sorts of things that can cause trouble in marriages if one is not prepared. Your child, for one thing, will know that he or she doesn't have to tolerate physical abuse. They will have such high self-esteem that if their spouse even gave an inkling of mistreating them, they would put a halt to it immediately. They will realize it's even preferable to be single, than to be mistreated.

Terri dated Guill eight years before marriage. Traci dated Jeff about three years. I have never seen either couple argue. They have never once complained an iota about their husbands. In fact, they reassure me how happy they are, and how well Guill and Jeff treat them. That's such a relief for me; just to know my girls are well taken care of and loved.

You know, I am now rather selfish. When I get discouraged about something, Terri, Traci and Tami are my best friends and supporters. I'm getting back what I taught and gave them. Often I've received cards from them telling me how much they appreciated the sacrifices I made for them. Gosh, I didn't even know they noticed, least of all, I didn't even realize I was sacrificing. One card told me 'how the mother is the key to keeping the family together' and my daughter told me I did just that. As the single parent, I get all the credit for how happy the girls are. I am now receiving the accolades continually. I so often hang up the phone from talking to one of them and I just start crying because I am so happy for them. As a single mother, I gave to this world three happy, loved, self-confident people who will give to this world a more decent environment. They will also contribute through their children to make the next generation a more superior one. We single parents could change the world. We can make right the wrong in this world. We are smart enough to know that this world needs people who are happy, loved, educated and with a high self-esteem. We can raise our children to grow up in that manner. Our society doesn't need more people spending hours and money in the psychologist and therapists offices and in the bars. We single parents have more time to be better parents, as we don't have a spouse demanding our attention. Can't you remember the times when you were married and you wanted to do something for your child or perhaps you had this great idea, but your spouse said, "That's silly. That won't make a difference. Forget it"? So, you dropped the subject and were angry with yourself. You knew you were right with your suggestions. Now is the time for you to do it. As a single parent, you can do anything you want. You will get so much praise and recognition from the world. Be consistent and unselfish. Your rewards will be countless, and they will continue down through your grandchildren. Your children will probably have left the house by the time you are 45 or 50 years old and there will be lots of time for you to do just any ole' thing you want. In fact, your children will encourage you to do things you have never thought of doing. They'll think you deserve it and want you to be so happy. Terri and Traci are so happy and all they want now is for me to find that special man and have a wild and crazy time. Hmmm!!

These rewards are unbeatable. They are lasting and I don't have to share them with anyone. The years I spent being a single parent have been much easier for me than those few years I was married and always trying to make the husband happy. I wouldn't trade my situation for any other.

SPECIAL THANKS

A special thanks to those who greatly helped and encouraged me to write this book:

Joe Murray -- The first person I called, whom I found in the Yellow Pages, associated with a publishing company in Hawaii. He told me, 'You can do it' and gave me many suggestions and positive encouragement.

My mother, Cathy Tyler, who no matter what I do, is always there for me and thinks I am the best daughter. Of course, to my three daughters and two sons-in-law, who have proven that all my efforts were worth while and they made my life so rewarding. My best female friends who listened and reminded me, when I would feel sorry for myself and be discouraged, that my children were my priorities. They gave me the words of praise to keep going. Shauna Uperesa, who spent that very first night with me in 1971 when I found out my husband was gone. She has known every emotion and thought I've gone through all these years as she has always been there for me. Then to my other best friends who would encourage me, make me laugh, invite me and the girls over to their house for holidays so I wouldn't be lonely or whatever: Barbara Wanamaker, Rory Claire, Gloria McFarlen, Ronalee MacQueen, Alice Newman, Sharon Waterhouse and the Sunday School Class of Hawaii Kai Baptist Church. My wonderful friends Anita and Roy Wold who truly saved my life and without them I might not be around to share this book with others (that's possibly another book I can write some time). My best male friends who one way or another helped me financially so that I could take the time to write this book -- Gordon Hartley, Eric Litaker, Cloyd Harris, Dr. Jon Wilson a Presbyterian minister and Joseph Ortiz. Then my grateful thanks go the following kids who were always there to greet me with a cheerful smile and make me realize that kids are the greatest creation God gave to us -- Kelly Scott, Allison Bohnen, Vicki Phillips, Adrianne Humiston, Stephanie Butler, Jason Saelzler, Steve Garcia, Lani Bobay, Amy Sullivan, Jenn Covell, Rebecca Eagle, Kara Lockhart, Malia Seltzer, Kealoha Seltzer, Robbie Shaffer, Nicholas McFarlen, Taryn Uperesa, Erin Murray, R.J. Powell, Jono Spaulding, Bridget Bohnen, Jen Hahl and Zach Terflinger,

I couldn't have written this without each and everyone of you. Thank you so much.

ABOUT THE AUTHOR

The author of this book, Ginger Lum, is a single parent who has raised three children alone, most of their growing years all by herself and she has *completed* the task successfully. People, even families with two parents, would often ask her how she did it. One day she began to actually think how she had done it and she realized that she really enjoyed all those years raising the children even with all the trials. She also realized there were some basic guidelines she had applied to her parenting. Her desire is to share with you as the reader some of the things she did with the hope to encourage other single parents.

All other books on the market that give suggestions for parents, whether they be single or married, have been written by psychologists, family counselors or ministers. These professional people are giving you their theory of what they **think** will work. There are a couple books, authored by an actual parent, however their job is not done yet. Their children are still young and these parents are not able to prove to the reader how well their children will turn out when they become teenagers and later when they are full grown and out on their own. Ginger wants to tell what she did and how she has proven it works as her three children are grown - out of college, show evidence of high self-esteem, happy, no bitterness and very able to make a substantial income.

Even though Ginger has written several articles, this is her first book. She wrote this book from a personal experience as a successful single parent. When she had her babies she made a conscious decision to raise her children so they would grow up with high self esteem, have the best education possible and be happy people, caring about others. She thought of these things daily as she raised her children. She didn't just leave things to chance. Her way worked! Her children never took drugs, drank, sassed or failed to do well in school. They are all smart, pretty, feel good about themselves and she says, "were fun to raise."

When Ms. Lum married she never dreamed she would be raising children alone. All she ever wanted was to be was a "good wife and mother." Desertion by her husband, after seven years, caused the marriage to end. She was 28 years old and had no college education She had been a stay at home mom, until the last four months when she began working as a teller at a bank Her husband left her with no money, no savings, no insurance, no assets and the checking account was over drawn. The car was repossessed one week later and she lived in low income housing. However, she was determined that she would not let this tragedy ruin her efforts to raise her children to grow up feeling loved, secure about themselves, educated and specifically not hating men because their dad had left them.

Ginger's friends gave her much sympathy after the girl's dad deserted them. The girls were 2 and 6 years old when they took daddy to work one day. When they went to pick him up at 5:00 p.m., they were all excited as they were going to see the movie *Pinocchio* that evening. However, daddy couldn't be found. These same people who once gave her sympathy now stand amazed and give her praise continually as they marvel at how well and happy her children have turned out. Over and over, she is asked by single people, as well as married people, "How did you raise your children to turn out so well?" People see her with her girls and will notice that they are smart, personable, pretty, and that they treat her with love and respect. She didn't think much about it as it seemed so natural. However, she began to think seriously about these comments, particularly when friends who had known her from that day when she was deserted, would seem surprised that her children had grown up and turned out so well, in spite of growing up in a single family home. On the other hand, Ginger would often feel sorry for many families, as she knew they have not been as fortunate with their children. She began to think that perhaps she could give some suggestions and be able to help other single parents. She wants others to enjoy their children as much as she did and she wants them to have the same excellent results. Often she even feels guilty because her girls gave her so much joy and no trouble. Ginger thought that if she could just encourage other single parents then this book would be worth it. Ginger Lum is confident that it can be much easier than you think and it can be so much fun raising children - if it is done right with a little extra thought.

Ginger's oldest daughter Terri is 35 years old and is a Pharmacist who works one day a week in a hospital in San Diego. The rest of the week she is a stay at home mom, while her husband, Guill has his own successful computer business. Terri and Guill, have two children and own their home in San Diego. Her second daughter, Traci, is 31 years old and graduated from Pepperdine University where she met her husband. They live in San Jose where they own their home and Traci is a stay at home mom and enjoys their two children. Jeff works in the computer business in the Silicon Valley area. Her youngest Tamalani (Tami) is 23 and in her second year at Pepperdine Law School. Tamalani is the daughter of a second husband who Ginger had a brief marriage with after being alone for five years. The second marriage didn't work and she divorced him and she had three children then to raise instead of two. She was glad she had that second marriage, even though it didn't last, because she was able to have another child to bring her much joy and pride and this child she could try her system out on child raising – and - it worked again.

Since her two older daughters have been out of high school and are married, they have never come to her with any problems or complaints. Why? Because they have high self esteem, they are well educated, they married on their own educational level and they had their goals. If they ever have any problems they know how to work things out amongst themselves. Tamalani is doing just as well in Law School and has a year and a half before she graduates.

After Ginger's husband left her, when she was 28 years old, she decided she only wanted to work part time, as she was worried about being available, for the potentially insecure little girls, as much as she could. She had to go on welfare for temporary help and she began to attend Real Estate School. She was very insecure and scared to death, as she had no higher education, training and couldn't even type, however she was determined that she wanted to get off welfare and be able to support her girls. She passed the real estate exam and was very soon able to get off welfare. Ginger has no doubt that if she could raise her kids to turn out so well, with her background, no college education; with no financial support from her ex husband and none from her parents, then you can too.